The Life on Other Worlds Series is a selection of classic accounts of the afterlife and otherworldly life, told by those who are already there or who have been shown glimpses of what awaits us when our lives on earth are over. Descriptions vary, yet a thread of similarity runs through them all. May this collection serve as a travel guide as we embark on the greatest adventure of all—the journey into the mysterious realms beyond this world.

*

OTHER VOLUMES IN THE SERIES INCLUDE
Earths in the Universe (1758) Emanuel Swedenborg
The Realms Beyond (1878) Paschal Beverly Randolph
A Wanderer in the Spirit Lands (1896) Franchezzo
Intra Muros (1898) Rebecca Ruter Springer
Two Years in Heaven (1911) Rose the Sunlight
The Life Beyond the Veil (4 Vols.) (1920-21) G. Vale Owen
Spiritual Life on Mars (1920) Eros Urides
The Blue Island & Other Spiritualist Writings (1922) William T. Stead
The World Unseen (3 Vols.) (1954-59) Anthony Borgia

The ANGELS' DIARY

AND
CELESTION STUDY OF MAN

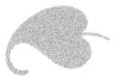

EFFIE M. SHIREY
and
CHARLES SAMSON

Through the hand of Elizabeth Maud Weatherhead

SQUARE CIRCLES PUBLISHING

The Angels' Diary
and
CELESTION STUDY OF MAN

By Effie M. Shirey and Charles Samson
Through the hand of Elizabeth Maud Weatherhead
© 1903 by Mrs. J. A. Seeds Samson Lender

Rechaptered version copyright © 2013
Square Circles Publishing

Cover: Syrp & Co.
Cover Art: "Angel" by Fra Angelico (1387-1455)

SQUARE CIRCLES PUBLISHING
P.O. Box 9682, Pahrump, NV 89060
www.SquareCirclesPublishing.com

eISBN: 978-0-9893962-3-3
ISBN: 978-0-9893962-6-4

Dedication

To Our Beloved Mother

Accept our offering from above,
Written in the Name of Love
May it go forth and bear good seed
To darkened homes and souls in need.
May it point the way that leads to light,
Filling men's souls with Godly might.
And some day in the courts divine
The book's good work a gem shall shine.

Contents

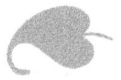

	DEDICATION	v
	ACKNOWLEDGMENT	ix
	PREFACE	x

THE ANGELS' DIARY

1	Transition	1
2	Reception	7
3	Heavenly Mansion	11
4	Return to Earth	17
5	Life in the Spheres	23
6	The Celestial Life	27
7	Through the Gates of Paradise	35
8	Grand Review of Angels	40
9	Paradise of God	44
10	Spiritual Type of Jesus	52
11	A Trip to the Sun	55
12	A Trip Through Space	59

CELESTION STUDY OF MAN

1	Nature of Man	65
2	Soul of Man	68
3	Power of Thought	71
4	Development of Soul Powers	75
5	Wonders of the Inner Organism	77

6	Significance of Color Vibrations	81
7	Dualistic Forces Harmonized	84
8	Physical and Psychical Non-Transmutable	88
9	Soul Progressive, Not Retrogressive	92
10	Immortality of the Soul	98
11	Communications on the Heavenly Life	106
12	Books and Their Writers	111
13	Music	117
14	Inspiration	121
15	New Thought Movement	126
16	Trinity	131
17	The Holy Ghost	133
18	A Treatise on Molecules	138
19	A Christmas Sermon to Humanity	142

Acknowledgment

This book, written by my beloved children, I present to the world with the earnest desire that all who read may receive "the peace that passeth understanding" and the Joy of Knowledge, Health and Wealth of Spirit.

There is in my soul the deepest feeling of gratitude for the inestimable benefit and service rendered through the marvelous powers of Elizabeth Maud Weatherhead. It was through her Hand that my dear son and daughter communicated from the Celestial Spheres the beautiful and instructive messages of this book.

Mrs. Julia A. Seeds Samson Lender
Denver, Colorado

Preface

The writers of this book pray that it may go forth upon its mission of love bearing a message of hope, cheer and encouragement to the homes of humanity. Its teachings shall be to bring light to the world, to show men the true way to immortality, to draw the curtain that swings between the Finite and the Infinite and to remove the sting of death, giving in its place the glorious reality of life beyond the tomb.

Oh, readers, take to your souls its heaven-born message and profit by its teachings. Learn from its pages that life upon the physical plane is but a shadow of the glorious life beyond. Learn that the change called "Death" is but the stepping-stone to higher and grander truths than those upon the physical plane. Learn that death is but the gateway where we lay our burdens down to take up a grand work in Heaven.

We pray that this book may teach men to look into their own souls, and there commune with God, the Creator and Giver of all life.

To those who have dear ones on the other side, look up and read the heavenly message. Your loved one has passed to that higher school of Universal Love and Progression. In that life of glorious possibilities, the soul shall unfold like a beautiful flower in the grand light of divine love. The little child who has flown like a bird from the home-nest shall be led by guardian angels in the heavenly land safe from the trials and temptations of the material world, and when its mother beholds it in the years to come it will be no longer a child, but a being glorious in beauty and strength, an Angel of Immortality.

To those who have struggled through the trials of physical life with but little to cheer and encourage them—there is a grand promise, *the promise, all that can make life desirable in the world beyond where things are seen as they really are, and not as they merely appear to be.*

We pray that the teachings of this book may furnish food for thought to all men. Not that the lesson will be the same to each reader, we know, but we ask that it may do good to all; that it may lift the shadow from troubled hearts, that it may sow good seed in the soul of the unbeliever, furnishing him with food for thought. That it may give new encouragement and hope to the discouraged, and the promise of eternal health to those who have become weakened in mind and body. This is the earnest wish and desire of the authors. May it go forth and bear good results.

By the Authors

Part One

THE ANGELS' DIARY

BY
Effie M. Shirey
of the Celestial Spheres

One

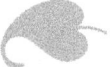

Transition

It must have been last night that I passed from earth and now today I am in this strange and wonderful place that charms me with its harmony, peace and beauty. In the world where I dwelt but yesterday, it was cold and cloudy and the ground was carpeted thickly with snow. Today is summer, flowers are blooming everywhere, the air is sweet with fragrance and countless numbers of birds are flitting from tree to tree singing their songs of gladness. How strange it all seems! Shall I wake up presently and find that I have been dreaming? I hope not. I think of the dear ones that I left behind—are they grieving for me, I wonder? Oh! if they could but know of the beautiful country that is now my abode!

What strange sensations were mine as I was passing from my physical body! It seemed as though I was being gradually lifted out of a case in which I had been placed and all the while it was as though I was passing under the influence of some anesthetic. Then the next thing I knew, I felt something snap and I stood outside of my material body that was now dead to the world. I was clothed in soft white garments and my long black hair fell far over my robe. There was a sense of buoyancy in my limbs that I had not felt since I was a little child. This was certainly interesting and I longed to investigate what was before me. I was soon floating away to where I knew not. I only knew that I felt strong, well and happy to be freed from pain. I could see many strange and beautiful sights as I floated through the air. One beautiful being that accompanied me told me that she was my guardian spirit and had been with me ever since I came into the world. The air seemed to be filled with angels and spirits; some were going to the earth upon various missions, others were returning to the heavenly and spiritual world. The atmosphere was filled with flowers, trees and various forms of vegetation, the spiritual parts of flowers, trees and foliage of the material plane. I wanted to stop and examine everything that I saw, but as this would require too long a time, I interested myself in taking glimpses of the things that we passed.

I could not measure the time, for to spiritual eyes there was no darkness, except once, and that was when we passed through the section that divides the spiritual from the material world. For a while there was nothing, absolutely nothing, and then we emerged into a beautiful region. The scenery was the most beautiful that I ever beheld, quite different from anything I had ever seen in material life. Presently we came to a region where the road branched off in two directions. I then learned that one road led to the spiritual world and the other to the heavenly regions. That which led to the heavenly realms was the more beautiful of the two; but no soul upon his first journey to the spiritual realms could pass over the path that leads to heaven; that was reserved for those who had progressed, developed and unfolded to the state of angelhood.

Over its entrance gleamed a beautiful gateway that seemed to be inlaid or studded with different colored stars, and overhead in letters of fire gleamed these words, *"Lay down your burdens, ye who enter here."*

How interesting it was to watch the people who passed on their way to the Spirit World—such a stream of them, men, women and children, and all seemed to be so strong and well. The country over which I passed was very fertile. Flowers and foliage seemed to grow in abundance. The first sphere was much like the earth, only more highly spiritualized, and those who dwell in this sphere had not outgrown their material desires; therefore, this first sphere has been created in a way to produce harmony. Those who live there must be taught and helped to progress, after they had learned the lessons of the first sphere and were desirous of improvement, they could pass into the second sphere. I found as I journeyed on, objects and conditions seemed to improve; things became more beautiful, the climate was milder and more perfect. In the lower sphere there was some degree of heat and cold and some darkness, but these conditions gradually passed away; in the fourth sphere there was a perfect climate. The fifth sphere was my destination. I found a beautiful home awaiting me there, more beautiful than anything I had ever dreamed of, while upon this material plane.

I longed to investigate this new and wonderful life, and as I look out from the home to which I came only last evening, my thoughts are filled with wonder and delight. The dear little brother who passed to spirit life before I was born, I have met. He has grown into a fine, manly fellow. I think how proud his mother would be if she could see him. I believe that I shall spend many pleasant hours with him. Conditions seemed so wonderful and strange, I can but marvel at the wisdom of the

Creator in designing such a grand and beautiful world for His children after their trials upon the material plane. It seemed odd, but I have as yet seen no darkness in this beautiful sphere; everything seems tinted in soft lights, yet there are no sun, moon or stars.

My spiritual home is formed of spiritual material and is a brownish pink in color. It is large and imposing, set in the midst of tall trees, terraced banks and beautiful flower-gardens. The interior is in keeping with the grandeur of the exterior. The rooms contain many new and wonderful things that I never saw or dreamed of before. *I have discovered that in this world we do not sleep and never become weary or tired.*

As I sit here in this wonderful home my mind turns to the dear ones I have left on earth. What would they think, I wonder, could they see me here? I think that they would be surprised.

I must go soon to the earth plane to see my little children. They will not realize that I have left them. They are hardly old enough as yet.

It seems so strange to see my thoughts produce themselves in indelible form upon sheets of spiritual paper, formed from flowers. Just to think that by the action of my own thought, I can produce a book. Well, there are many strange and wonderful things before me. I long to know more of this wonderful life. The dear brother is coming presently to take me to a beautiful affair that is going on somewhere in this grand world. I am so enraptured with the thought and am so anxious.

In my Father's house are many mansions.

JESUS.

I stand in Eternity
 I lave in the ocean of Truth,
And bask in the Golden Sunshine
 Of Endless Love and Youth.

       Pittsinger.

Two

Reception

How beautiful life seemed. My soul was filled with gladness as I waited for my darling brother to come to me. I was glad to see his happy, smiling face, and soon we were walking together through the beautiful country that abounds in such new and wonderful scenery. I thought to myself, "It is winter upon the material plane and I have been transported suddenly into a Summerland." My soul was filled with joyful anticipation of what was to come. I was like a little child who knows no sorrow.

As we wandered along listening to the strains of delightful music which seemed to come from every direction, we met groups of white-robed angels talking with one another beneath the trees. Every one seemed to have caught the harmony that predominates in the beautiful Summerland. I was so happy and interested in all that I saw about me that I did not even ask my darling brother where it was that we were going. I felt content to wander on and on for any length of time amid such glorious scenes as I saw about me. Occasionally, the thought occurred to me, "Am I dreaming, and shall I suddenly wake up to the old life far away upon the earth?" Everything seemed to be so satisfying. It was beautiful to think of, to see every one provided for and no thought of envy or selfishness in any soul. We seemed to glide over the ground, our feet never touching it. Sometimes we appeared to be floating in the air, then again we were four or five inches above the ground. It was a very delightful sensation to move in this way, quite unlike walking in the material world.

I was surprised as we came to a clear, silvery lake with small flower-boats gliding over the surface to find myself walking upon the water. This was another new experience and seemed quite novel to me. After walking half way across the lake my darling brother said, *"Now we will walk through the water,"* and behold we were upon the bed of the lake below. We could look up and see the scenery above the surface of the water, and it seemed to me that in passing through this water I gained new spiritual strength, for when we emerged as dry as though we had only walked upon the land I was conscious of an improvement in my spiritual condition, and was reminded of the words, "Drink of the fountain of everlasting life and ye shall be white as snow." Occasionally we saw beautiful little summer houses or pagodas, covered with flowering vines, and then we would enter and view for a while the surrounding scenery. Nature certainly did look very beautiful bathed in the soft light that was sometimes rose-colored, sometimes blue, and then again the most brilliant, beautiful green that I had ever seen. We paid no heed to the lapses of time; indeed, there was no time in this beautiful world. Everybody was young and there was eternity to live in.

Presently we came to a beautiful grove, where great numbers of people were assembled. The trees seemed to be hung with festoons of brilliant flowers, and roses of different colors seemed to form a carpet for the feet. I wondered what kind of a gathering or fête it might be, and presently three beautiful angels came forward bearing in their arms a robe formed of delicate pink roses. As they came near they threw the robe over me, saying, "*Welcome, dear heart,*" and then I learned that the relatives of my father and mother for several generations back had gathered here in a reunion to celebrate the advent of a new number to the heavenly land. I was the new member and the guest of honor upon this occasion. I thought of my darling mother and wished that she might have seen me in that pink flower-robe with my long black hair failing nearly to my feet. (My spiritual hair is much longer and more abundant than the hair that had adorned my head in material life.) Surely, I thought, it would make anybody wish to pass to this higher life could they know how wonderful it is.

The festivities that followed were beautiful indeed, and there were many things that were entirely beyond the comprehension of a material mind. One beautiful angel, whose name I learned to be Alice Samson, sang most beautifully. I never in my years of life had heard such a magnificent voice. The memory of those tones will linger in my mind throughout all time. As she sang the listeners threw beautiful flowers at her, forming a brilliant-hued platform about her. It was very beautiful and inspiring, and filled me with a delight that I had never experienced. In the center of the grove upon a table formed of white roses, was spread all sorts of spiritual food in the way of fruit, and deep flower-cups held the spiritual liquid.

Eye hath not seen, nor ear heard, neither have entered into the heart of man, the things which God hath prepared for them that love Him. But God hath revealed them unto us by His Spirit.

St. Paul.

Three

Heavenly Mansion

It was certainly very delightful to be the honored guest in such beautiful company. It seemed to me that I had never been quite so happy.

The liquid and fruit that I tasted filled me with a new sensation that I had never experienced before.

I was continually wondering what new surprise awaited me. I could see a soft and beautiful light emanating from the persons about me. I learned that it was the electric ether showing the spirituality of the individuals, the light surrounding some being more than that of others. The spiritual food I learned did not build up any portion of the spiritual body; it only helped to increase the higher vibrations, making the individual more spiritual.

A procession composed of tiny angels wearing flower-robes and bearing festoons of flowers was very pretty indeed. I thought of the mothers whose little children had been taken to this beautiful world, and it seemed to me that if they only knew they would not grieve so much for their little ones.

There in the beautiful grove I took in the grand picture before me—the white-robed angels in their flowing hair and white, cloud-like garments; the little children floating, gliding through the air and showering down their armfuls of fragrant flowers; then the soft-tinted light that shone upon the scene, changing continually to the most beautiful colors, many of which I had never beheld before. Such peace, such harmony seemed to abound, and the dear brother whispered to me, "Sister, you have heard of 'that peace that passeth understanding'—it is that which you experience now; it is the peace of heaven which the world cannot give." It seemed so delightful to be in the midst of such beautiful scenery and pleasant company, and feel that time was not passing and one would not have to think of some duty that might call him away.

After delightful music, vocal and instrumental, and several interesting talks by different members of the company, all were invited to meet in the palatial home of Joseph Samson. This was a palace of grandeur, a short distance from the grove where the festivities had been held. The building itself appeared to be formed of crystal with a soft light over it like the colors of an opal. There were no doors to the building, but it was a very easy matter to glide in through the walls. The interior of the mansion exceeded my brightest dreams or imaginings of palatial grandeur. Down the center of the building was a long archway about fifty feet wide, and a marble fountain in the form of an angel throwing up sprays of fragrant colored water. Red lotus flowers were growing in the basin of the fountain, and gorgeous-hued butterflies and birds of brilliant plumage were fluttering about like flashes of brilliant light.

The long archway itself seemed to be formed of electricity. I learned that the occupants of this delightful mansion were ancestors of my father and had been many years in the heavenly world and were very highly spiritualized individuals. Upon either side of the archway just mentioned were pictures upon the crystal walls, many of which I could not understand. They did not appear to be paintings, for they kept changing to different scenes. As I was trying to fathom the mystery, a scholarly-looking angel in a white tunic belted at the waist said to me, "Think of something that you would like to see reproduced." I thought at once of the dear mother far away upon the earth plane, and lo, her picture in life size appeared upon the crystal walls. This was something very novel and new to me, and for quite a while I interested myself in producing pictures.

As I said before, I saw pictures that I could not understand; they were the thoughts and soul-pictures of the spiritual beings who passed through this place, many of whom had been developing and unfolding for thousands of years. It occurred to me that one should be very careful of his thoughts and train himself to high and lofty ideas.

It was delightful to be privileged to enter such a place. It seemed to me that I must be worthy or I would not be permitted, but still I could not but wonder how one who had so lately passed from earth with naturally many weaknesses should be privileged to meet here with such highly developed beings.

After passing through the long archway we came to the gallery of art, where there are works of art from many of the great masters—Michelangelo, Murillo and others who had never lived upon the material plane. Never in my life had I looked upon such magnificent works of art. The paintings had been produced upon the walls and were not hung there. About each picture were brilliant stars of different colors, and these made a sort of frame to the picture as well as showed it in its proper light; some pictures requiring a blue light, others rose color and still others a soft, mellow, yellow light. What a place this is for the lover of art! I thought to myself how happy must have been the artist who was privileged to produce the work of his soul amid such peace and exquisite harmony.

One picture that I admired very much was entitled "The Eternal Judgment," showing the love of God. It seems that Michelangelo, while he was on earth, painted a masterpiece at Rome entitled "The Last Judgment." In that picture he depicted the wrath of God upon the Day of Judgment. After Angelo passed to the spiritual world he saw that he had made a mistake in painting his "Last Judgment," and so whenever he might be permitted in the homes of heaven he produced a heavenly masterpiece showing the love and compassion of God for his weak and erring children. I must not take too long a time in describing the pictures, for there were many of them, many thousands in fact, and it would be impossible to enumerate them all.

Leading out from this gallery of art were the rainbow rooms. These rooms were arranged in the form of a rainbow, being formed of the colors violet, indigo, blue, green, yellow, orange and red. The violet room was inlaid with amethysts. They were set so closely together as to form a broad arch of solid amethysts. The next room was set with dark blue jewels, having the shape of diamonds. The third room was of light blue jewels. The fourth was of emeralds. The fifth of yellow topaz. The sixth of a deep orange jewel whose name I did not know, and the seventh was formed of garnets and rubies. The interior of each of these rooms was of the same color as the exterior and beautiful jewels shed their light upon the articles to be found in these rooms. What a wonderful home this is!

I was continually wondering what new wonder was to appear before me. The music room and concert hall were very inspiring with the tones of soft, melodious music vibrating frequently, with no hands touching the instruments. I learned that one had but to sing an air to himself and immediately the vibration would be produced upon the delicate-toned instruments and they played music sweeter, softer and finer than any ever heard upon an instrument of earth. I began to see now the wonderful powers of the spiritual mind, unhampered by the physical.

I was interested in the Scientific Laboratory of this magnificent home. Here all the wonders of science were made clear; electricity was explained and how it works; the difference between magnetism and electricity; how inspiration was given to a material brain by an angelic being; the birth and evolution of a thought; gravitation and many, many things that I cannot explain in writing. Many scientists of heaven were gathered in this laboratory, and when they had worked out some wonderful idea they immediately took it to the earth plane and gave it to Tesla, Flammarion, Edison or some other inventor by way of inspiration. It was certainly very wonderful to learn of the many forms of electricity. I saw many scientific problems worked out successfully that the material world will not be ready for for many a day.

It seemed that I spent days in that delightful home, but there was nothing to indicate the flight of time—no weariness, no darkness, or no hunger. It was certainly very delightful. It was like a vivid, beautiful dream. The people that I met inspired me with their intellectual force and spiritual ability. It will certainly be very helpful to me, I thought, to have had this experience. One other very interesting room contained collections gathered from the higher spheres, many of which I have never formed the slightest conception of before. Later on in my writings I will explain this celestial room.

"Someday," we say, and turn our eyes
 Toward the fair hills of Paradise;
Some day, some time, a sweet new rest
 Shall blossom, flower-like, in each breast;
Some day, some time, our eyes shall see
 The faces kept in memory;
Some day their hand shall clasp our hand,
 Just over in the Morning-land—
O Morning-land! O morning-land!

Phelps.

Four

Return to Earth

The impressions produced upon my spiritual mind during my visit to that delightful mansion in the heavenly world were so deep and lasting that I shall be able to recall them through all the years of eternity. All the while I was enjoying myself I could feel vibrations sent from the dear mother far away upon the earth plane. I felt within my soul that the time would come when I would be able to reveal myself to her and tell her of my new and wonderful life in the heavenly world. My soul was filled with thanksgiving and I thanked the Creator of all life for my existence. I thought if one might go on forever in such delightful harmony what a pleasure it would be to live. Already I felt my spiritual mind expanding and growing in my new and beautiful life. It did me good to look at my dear brother so grand and imposing in appearance; I wished that his mother might see the child whom she gave to heaven at a tender age, grown into a tall, handsome angel with a grand head crowned in masses of waving black hair. I wondered if he would have looked so imposing in appearance if he had not had the opportunities that had been given him to unfold and develop in the Spirit World.

We spent many hours in the delightful home I have mentioned, and as we passed out to return once more to my own new and beautiful home my mind was filled with wondering thoughts. There was so much before me still to learn, so much to assimilate in my spiritual mind. It seemed as though I had spent the most delightful afternoon of my life; in reality I had spent, according to material time, several days. My soul felt as though it had wings and the thought occurred to me that I must return to earth and if possible send out some helpful vibrations to the dear ones who were grieving for me there. The dear brother decided to accompany me and we set out for the journey. Of course, my brother had made the trip many times, so it was not so much of a novelty to him as it was to me. I felt that I had gained much since passing from my physical body and my soul rejoiced in the fact.

It was a different route over which we passed from the one by which we entered. We entered by way of the Spirit World, but upon this occasion we passed through the angelic spheres and out of the beautiful gate. I was delighted with all that I saw before me, and was as interested as I had been before my entrance into the wonderful country. It seemed to me that I had never looked upon such beautiful flowers as were growing everywhere. I could see the fruit trees upon one side, pink and white with blossoms, and upon the other side many varieties of fruit all upon one variety of tree. The grapes seemed so odd to me, many of them no smaller than good-sized apples, but possessing neither outside skin nor seed of any kind. People upon the material plane might ask how they held together without skin or seed. If they could understand the laws and forces by which spiritual elements are governed they would not wonder at such a thing.

Upon my journey I witnessed phenomena that I could never have possibly imagined had I possessed only material knowledge. The angelic, spiritual and heavenly worlds were all radiant with light as we passed through, and the beautiful gateway glowed in the soft, peaceful atmosphere of heaven. Never shall I forget the picture that greeted my eyes as I stood upon what seemed to be a boundary line between the material universe and the world of angels and spirits. I could see the mighty universe pass before me not like a panorama, for it did not pass out of my sight for an instant. There I could see the sun in all its heat and magnitude, a great sphere of blazing light, larger than anything I had ever imagined. Then the planets and the millions and millions of stars in more colors and tints than it is possible for the material mind to comprehend. They certainly did look very beautiful.

One brilliant blue star many times larger than a house would be set in the center of a circle of twinkling rose-colored satellites. Then there would be clusters of bright green stars surrounded by larger clusters of yellow stars, and these would be encircled by deep red stars that flashed and twinkled in a thousand vibrations. Then I could see how the vibrations of the stars and the atmosphere around them had its effect upon the people of the physical plane, for some active stars were sending out vibrations that I could see strike the earth many millions of miles away. I could see what effect intense vibrations from the planet Mars had upon the people of the earth, as well as the blue vibrations from Saturn. Venus sent out pink vibrations and those from the sun were both red and yellow, and from other planets the vibrations would be white, and when two vibrations crossed as they were sent to the earth there was apt to be disturbance of some kind in the earth's atmosphere. And sometimes thousands of vibrations would strike the minds of men, causing them to get into a state of intense excitement, not knowing how such conditions existed.

I thought the moon a very queer looking place with its hollow volcanic mountains and its peculiar wind blowing continually. I thought the picture of the universe, the stars and the constellations, the comets and flashes of light, meteorites and many other sights lost to the material eye the most beautiful and wonderful sight it had ever been my lot to witness. It was night to the people of the material plane, but not to me, a spiritual being, and one strange sight that struck me as being very peculiar was this: In the particular place where I was bound for, the physical bodies of the inhabitants were asleep, while the astral form of the individual was free to wander wheresoever it willed, and from every embodied spirit was a long stream of light, the life-force connected with the physical body, which was at rest and in preparation for the work of the next day. I was glad to have it this way, for the astral forms of my dear ones were able to see me and I could talk to them as I could not have done had they been in the normal waking state. They never knew just when the physical body would pull upon the life-cord drawing the astral back into the body; in this case we would be obliged to part for a while. I was glad, however, to have a good talk with the dear mother and to tell her not to grieve for me when she awoke, and found me gone.

The material plane itself seemed quite inferior to the new country I had found, still it was the abiding place of those I loved and as such was worthy of my loving interest. I was interested in embodied and disembodied spirits as I saw them meet in loving communion upon the astral. To many whose lives were hard and unpleasant in the waking state it was the only source of pleasure that they had and made a bright spot that could not fail to be appreciated.

Not all the archangels can tell
    The joys of the holiest place,
Where the Father is pleased to reveal
    The light of His heavenly face.

Wesley.

Five

Life in the Spheres

I did not fail to visit all of my dear ones, and returned to the Spirit World regretting that the inhabitants of the material plane could not all know of the grand and beautiful life in the beyond. It was such a delight to realize that I could go anywhere that I desired, and that I had the privilege to visit any point on earth, in the Spirit World or heaven. *"Surely,"* thought I, *"the change called death is but a higher birth and a condition very much to be desired."*

There were crowds of people journeying to and from the earth; I could see many little children, some so tiny that they had to be borne in the arms of their guardian angels. It was a novelty to the spirit-children, who could not realize of course that they were now dead to the world, and were journeying toward a new land where they would grow and unfold in wisdom, knowledge and beauty. It was interesting to see the children who had been crippled and blind and who were now able to see and walk for the first time. They could scarcely contain themselves, they were so happy. They seemed like little birds who had just found their wings. It was not a pleasant sight to come in contact with those who had passed out of the body sinful and wicked. I was pleased to see that many of the so-called undeveloped spirits were being taught in the lower spheres, and that they were endeavoring to reach the way to progression by helping themselves through the aid of others to a higher plane of understanding.

Upon my return trip I desired to visit each sphere and to learn the laws by which the Creator's large family were kept in such a state of harmony and good will. There were many undeveloped spirits wandering about the earth and there were others confined in the dark sphere, but there was hope for all, and as there was no satisfaction to them in such a life the majority would after a time endeavor to (by their good work and the desire for something higher) reach the first sphere, and after they had learned the lesson of this sphere and could impart the knowledge to some other spirit who was anxious to enter the first sphere, they could then pass up into the second sphere and so on up through the different spheres. I found that each individual occupied his proper place and so in this way harmony prevailed. An undeveloped spirit did not dwell in the spheres with those whose desires were purely spiritual. In the fourth sphere a spirit becomes an angel, and with this step he had conquered all material tendencies or selfish characteristics. The fifth sphere is the sphere of family love. Families wait in this sphere for many years for their loved ones to pass to spirit life. I liked the sixth sphere; everything there is so bright and beautiful.

My new life had only begun now and I was anxious to take up the duties of such a life. I was glad to learn that I could take up any line of study that I desired and could improve and perfect myself in many branches of learning if I would only apply myself. I decided to do this and my life became a very busy one, but this did not prevent me from visiting each day my father, mother, husband and children. There seemed to be no limitation of time in that grand and beautiful world. Since we did not sleep and there was no night, there was plenty of time for study. I was delighted with my own beautiful home, and new pleasures were continually awaiting me. I was anxious to perfect myself in music and art, and I lost no time in taking these up. I was also interested in scientific investigation and very much so in the instructive lectures delivered by learned men in the great hall of science in the Celestial Sphere.

I was much interested in the children's homes. They appeared like great marble palaces and within were thousands of little children being reared and educated under the law of divine love. I saw there the tiniest sparks of life, who had never opened their eyes to material things but had been brought here to grow up in knowledge, love and wisdom. All infants were able here to walk and move, but not all could ascend and descend; that was a power which they would all acquire after being there a short time. In the beautiful homes I have mentioned were to be found many guardian angels as well as kind-souled women whose life tendencies were toward the caring for and bringing up of little children. It was a very happy thought to realize how well God's children were provided for. One sphere many times larger than the earth was called the Sphere of Purity; everything was white in this sphere, the buildings, the ground, the grass, the foliage upon the trees and all the flowers. A person might understand from this description that the Sphere of Purity might appear cold and lifeless; such was not the case; it was most beautiful with a soft, rose-colored light shining over its dazzling beauty.

And I heard a great voice out of heaven saying: Behold the tabernacle of God IS within men and He will dwell with them and they shall be His people and God himself shall be with them AND BE their God. And God shall wipe away all tears from their eyes, and there shall be no more death, neither sorrow nor crying, neither shall there be any more pain, for the former things are passed away.

Revelations 21:3-4.

Six

The Celestial Life

How beautiful it is to be an inhabitant of such it wonderful land! This fact became more deeply impressed upon my mind as I grew and unfolded in my new life. I found a great deal to interest me in each sphere and it seemed that there was always something new to charm my sight and hearing. I was so happy, and how I longed for the time when I could carry the heavenly message to the dear ones far away on the earth! The dear brother was a continual delight to me; he seemed during his years in the heavenly world to have absorbed a wealth of knowledge, and then he was such an inspiring teacher. I was never weary of learning from him.

After a time the new life became so natural to me that it seemed as though I had always known it; it was no longer a dream but a grand and beautiful reality. With my studies, my music and art, the companionship of new friends that I had found since I became an inhabitant of the heavenly world, the delightful musicales and instructive lectures, the time passed very pleasantly. Shortly after passing over I was brought into the presence of that grand character who is known to the world as the Savior. I was deeply impressed with his tenderness and gentle manner, and his presence was such as to inspire one with the desire to be good and true. After coming in contact with this purely spiritual character I felt stronger and better than I ever had before. It was an inspiration that remained within my soul.

I was delighted with a visit made to the home of Michelangelo in the Celestial Sphere. The works of art were most magnificent, and this visit only added another delightful reminiscence to my store of beautiful experiences. It was so grand to think that one was not limited in his desires in this heavenly world. All homes, buildings, music hills, scientific laboratories and lecture halls were open to the public. There was always an instructive lecture to attend if one so desired, and the musicales and concerts were so inspiring. Those who had been limited on earth and who had desired to hear Jennie Lind[1] or Emma Abbott[2] sing could listen to their music in the music halls of heaven. There were all the poets, Longfellow, Whittier, Tennyson, Holmes, Bryant, Emerson, Goldsmith and others—all possessing magnificent homes and entertaining in royal style. Such a life as the one that I had found was certainly greatly to be desired. To think that one might go on through all eternity, receiving instruction, developing and unfolding in an atmosphere of the most elevated thought was a privileged greatly valued by those who were inmates of this wonderful world.

I spent many delightful hours in the home of my ancestor described during the early part of my spiritual life. The Celestial Chamber was a continual delight to me. The collection of

---

[1] JENNY LIND (1820–1887) was a Swedish opera singer.
[2] EMMA ABBOTT (1850–1891) was an American operatic soprano.

curious and beautiful creations furnished me with inspiring thoughts, such strange creations gathered from the Celestial Sphere. I sometimes wondered that I had the power to comprehend them. *I realized if certain senses in my soul had not been awakened after I had laid aside my physical body that I would not have been able to see the objects at all; they would have been as far from my comprehension as heaven or an angel would be beyond the comprehension of a worm of the dust.* I understood well that certain senses of the immortal soul remain in a dormant state while one is in the physical body, unless by deep thought and concentration they are awakened and brought into life. The awakening of these soul-senses will serve to make the physical plane a more beautiful and pleasant place than it is, and a great deal of sin, sorrow, pain and poverty could be done away, if the sixth, seventh and eighth senses were developed instead of only the first, second, third, fourth and fifth—the fifth[3] being dormant in a great many individuals. *What wonderful possibilities are folded away in the soul of an infant, and how carefully and tenderly these possibilities should be brought out, if one would improve the earthly conditions.*

There were many experiences through which I passed, and many objects that charmed my sight which would be utterly incomprehensible to the material mind if I should attempt to give a description of them. I must reserve them for some time in the future, when the mind of man has unfolded some of its latent powers. The Affairs of Heaven, the Grand Review of Angels, the Flower Carnival, the Celebration of Archangels, the Apostolic Festival, the Family Reunion and many others too numerous to mention, filled my soul with elevated thoughts. These things so far exceeded anything held

---
[3] Intellectual.

upon the material plane that there was no comparison. There were lessons to be found in all things if one would only see them by divine light and understanding.

It was not long after my entrance to the heavenly world that I held a reception in my own home; the soft, inspiring music, the beautiful lights, the spiritual faces of the angels, the flowing white robes and the loosened hair of my angelic guests formed a picture never to be forgotten by those who witnessed it. I was happier than I had ever been; how I wished that my babies, my darling mother and husband might have mingled with the guests as they glided through the rooms of my home, passing the time in music and pleasant thought. My angel brother was quite a lion upon this occasion; to look at him was an inspiration, and when he spoke my guests were charmed, so grand was his voice and so beautiful his spoken thoughts. Once again did I wish that his mother might see him. Such scenes were more beautiful than those witnessed upon the material plane, for the thoughts of all were pure and elevated and furnished food for the soul. I thought how different is this from the idea that people hold of the spiritual world being a place where the sanctified walk about a white throne singing hymns continually, and how much more satisfying to the active life of the spiritual body.

I was very glad that the Creator had designed his works in a way so thoroughly pleasing to his children. During my early experiences in the Spirit World I would try to comprehend the meaning of "Eternity" and finally it dawned upon my mind that I was living in eternity. *Eternity is today, and tomorrow is eternity, and throughout all time there is opportunity to grow nearer toward Godly perfection—nearer toward the truth, nearer toward complete happiness.* The very restlessness that causes the soul to soar upward either as an embodied or disembodied spirit is an indication of its higher growth. And so I thought what I learn now will prepare me for higher lessons that are to come later on, and my soul was so eager to acquire its daily lessons. As I grew and developed, I found more satisfaction in life than ever before. The experiences of my life were varied and there was no condition that I found monotonous. Early in the morning while the world which I visited was in sleep, I would go to my loved ones for a while and bring to them the vibrations from a better land. Sometimes they were receptive to these vibrations and at other times they could not receive my help in the smallest degree. Sometimes after leaving my loved ones I would take a short trip somewhere upon the earth.

I found a great deal to interest me, but there were no scenes so beautiful as those I could see in the heavenly world, and so I was always happy to return to them. A few hours spent with my studies, then more time in the pleasant companionship of dear friends, then a lecture or concert or the privilege of witnessing some scientific experiment soon to be given to the world through the brain of some receptive individual, and then after this, a pleasant walk over the beautiful grounds of my home with my beloved brother, my angelic guide or with my own soul. In the latter care, I would spend a pleasant hour in reflection and companionship with my own soul.

What a wonderful life it was; no time wasted, but all spent in helping the soul to grow and unfold its mighty powers. Sometimes it would be a visit to the lower spheres to help and instruct some undeveloped spirit who desired to rise, then again there would be a call to the earth plane to a scene of accident where many lives were to go out, some lives needing assistance to help them to the Spirit World. And so my life glided along, peacefully and pleasantly, through three years of spiritual life. I have gained much—my soul has grasped many lessons of truth and wisdom, but it is only in the beginning of spiritual knowledge. I trust that it may have many new and wonderful truths to tell you as this journal is continued, at some future date.

Thoughts of Heaven

I am sitting alone in the twilight
    In the hush of the closing day,
And a feeling of rapture steals o'er me
    And my thoughts they are far away.

I am thinking tonight of heaven,
    That beautiful land so fair;
Of the angels so pure and spotless,
    Who dwell in harmony there.

I have heard of that beautiful country
    That God in His wisdom has made;
I have heard of its joys supernal,
    Of its flowers that never fade.

I have longed to walk through that city—
    That beautiful land of my dreams
Where dross is not mixed with the golden
    And life there is just what it seems.

I have pictured often the Savior
    With His matchless face all aglow,
Walking among his disciples
    In raiment all white like the snow.

Lo! O'er my enraptured vision
    Comes a something that seems like a spell;
I have caught just a glimpse of that country
    Far away where the angels dwell.

I can hear the glad strains of their music
    As softly it comes floating near.
Oh! rapturous tones of heaven
    Falling so sweetly on my ear.

But alas! it has gone all too quickly;
    My vision of heaven is o'er,
And I think of life and its promise
    As I never had thought before.

And I think how far from God's purpose
    The most of our lives are led—
We are so weak, my Father,
    Calling to Thee for bread.

We should make life an example
    Strong with truth, faith and love;
Make our lives a structure
    That shall rise to the heights above.

Seven

Through the Gates of Paradise

Far away beyond the boundaries of the material plane is a glorious land—a land of eternal summer, where the fragrance of flowers floats softly upon the air. This beautiful land is the abode of those who have vacated the house of clay to take up their residence from now on through all eternity in a life of sweetest harmony and most perfect peace.

In this glorious Summerland are the many mansions not built by hands, but eternal in the Heavens; not built to crumble and decay, but created to endure through all time. Strains of rapturous music float soft and free over the fair green hills of this beautiful land. A beautiful gateway guards the entrance to Paradise that offers a wonderful promise to many whose spiritual eyes have been opened for the first time. It seems to speak of the promise to the soul—"Lay down your burdens, weary one, for here is perfect rest."

Paradise is the heaven that awaits God's fair blossoms—the little children who have blossomed on earth to bloom above. It is the abode of those who have laid aside the weaknesses of the material body. What glorious realities are to be found within that Paradise of the Blessed—such scenes as have never been imagined by the material mind; grand old trees bending down upon one side with different varieties of fruit and upon the other side a perfect mass of pink and white bloom, flower gardens whose equal has never been seen before. Not all the glorious wealth of floral beauty and vegetation of the tropics can be compared to that in the Summerland above. The beautiful colors that play softly upon the creations of Heaven add an indescribable beauty to the scene. There are rivers, lakes and mountains to be found in the eternal land, but they are as clear as crystal, and an inhabitant of that plane may walk through its waters and come forth strengthened and highly spiritualized. Small craft built of iridescent shells and festooned with lovely flowers glide dreamily over the surface of the water, the banks upon all sides being brilliant with tinted sand of various colors.

One may see angelic beings in white robes with loosely flowing hair gliding softly over the surface of the ground or floating leisurely through the air; some conversing with one another, others lifting the voice in song; some beautiful angelic beings bearing in their arms tiny babies who have been carried from the earth plane to this glorious land of mighty love and eternal peace. If the mothers of such little ones could only see, how differently they would feel.

The homes to be found in the eternal land are not of a sameness although all are lovely. There are small homes completely overgrown with flowering vines, and those who dwell within are there because they like such a home. They feel more content than they would in a fine mansion or gorgeous palace. There are co-operative homes where hundreds of people live together in the most perfect harmony without the drudgery of material work, all things being run upon the most approved plan—no cooking, no sweeping, no sewing or housework of any kind, for the spiritual body needs nothing of this kind.

There are homes devoted entirely to young people where a literary, social and musical life may be enjoyed by those dwelling within such a home. There are palaces and mansions for those who desire them. There are colleges of science where students work out mighty problems and experiments. Those interested in this line find their homes in such colleges, since the spiritual body never sleeps or becomes weary from its work. There are the mighty temples of art and music, the lecture halls, the beautiful homes for the children, and the palaces of the great writers and artists, where receptions are held daily, and where one may meet with noted people, as the great men and women of the eternal world are at work with the creations of their souls. Naturally, when a reception is held at the home of Beecher, Longfellow or any other gifted angel, the conversation drifts to the latest work of some great artist, poet, musician or inventor. Many things are discussed that the inhabitants of the material plane are not ready for yet, but will be some day when man has learned to develop his latent faculties. To those who are interested in such things instructive lectures are being given continually that furnish food for the soul desiring unfoldment. The works of art in the higher world are all upon pure and lofty subjects.

Frequently there are meetings where there is no lecturer present, he being somewhere in one of the spheres and sending his thoughts to the listeners, who are gathered together and who are enabled to hear every word without even a wireless telegraph. In many of the gatherings scenes that are transpiring in the different spheres are sent and transferred by means of vision that all may see through the power of the subconscious mind. There are many wonderful things that take place within the eternal city, events of which I shall speak at some future time.

Are they not all ministering spirits, sent forth to minister for them who shall be heirs of salvation?

ST. PAUL.

Eight

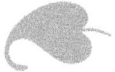

Grand Review of Angels

Beyond the boundary of the material world in the Celestial Sphere is situated the Temple of Light. It is the most magnificent creation ever raised in the name of God. It is made of opalescent material radiating every color of the rainbow. It sheds its tinted light upon all objects that are in its vicinity. It resembles a mighty palace of opal stone. Its dimensions are very spacious. It has towers, turrets and domes. Its columns are fluted and carved in beautiful design.

In this temple is held once a year the Grand Review of Angels. Upon this occasion all the inhabitants of the spiritual and heavenly worlds must gather in this temple to pass in Grand Review and receive the Gift of the Spirit, which will help them to progress during the coming year. Upon the occasion of the Grand Review of Angels, it is a very beautiful sight to see the inhabitants of the Spirit World coming from all directions to meet in one grand conclave in the Temple of Light; some floating through the air, others gliding along with feet that scarcely touch the ground, bearing garlands of flowers, or showering them over the pathway for those who are following in the rear.

All inhabitants of the Spirit World look forward to this occasion with much delight, as it certainly is very beautiful. If mothers who grieve for the little ones (who have left them to go, they know not where) could see them in the midst of all the grandeur and beauty of the Temple of Light, they would say, "It is well; my child is far better off than he would be amid the trials and temptations of the material world." The streams of white-robed angels and spirits as they pass into the temple through apparently closed walls is a sight never to be forgotten by those who have the privilege of witnessing it.

This temple, you understand, has been created just as have been the sun, moon and stars. It has been created to endure throughout all time. The ground surrounding the temple is in keeping with its grandeur; beautiful flowers, grand old trees, terraced banks, fountains carved in the form of angels sending up rainbow-tinted spray-scenes more beautiful than any material eye has ever witnessed.

The marvelous feature of the conclave is this: No matter how many millions of angels meet together, there is no crowding or pushing or straining of necks to see what is going on. The scene is visible to all eyes.

The music, from a choir composed of thousands of voices, is so harmoniously blended that there is not one harsh, discordant note, but only the most exquisite tones. Within the Temple of Light upon the occasion I have mentioned may be heard the most rapturous music. Heavenly instruments are played-by the power of vibrations, but the mighty organ, which occupies nearly a block in extent, is played upon by some of the masters—Handel, Beethoven, Mozart, Mendelssohn or some other angel equally skilled. Think of it! To hear such men play, or to hear Emma Abbott sing as she never sang in her life upon the material plane.

How grand to be privileged to enter the Temple of Light. The interior overhead is studded with hundreds of blue and rose-colored stars, soft rainbow-tinted lights bathe everything in a beautiful glow. Millions upon millions of angels are to be seen and yet there would be room for a million more if it were necessary. And when the mighty choir, composed of thousands of voices, joins in one grand burst of song the grandeur of the occasion is indescribable. Then every angel present is prepared to receive a blessing that will insure new strength in spiritual unfoldment. First come the little babies, pure and spotless as the newly-opened flower, then the children, and then the youth and maiden, and last those who have had years of material experience. All this scene is very grand and impressive and must be witnessed to be fully appreciated.

The ceremony ends in a grand burst of heavenly music and all pass out with joyful souls, thankful that they have been privileged to participate in the Grand Review of Angels. How glorious to be an angel, to know that you have eternity to perfect yourself in, to know that the trials of your life have all been laid away and from henceforth on all shall be glorious, beautiful and free! Truly those who pass to the spiritual side of life have gained a wonderful experience.

Let your light so shine before men that they may see your good works and glorify your Father which is in Heaven.

St. Matthew 5:16.

Nine

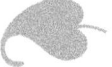

Paradise of God

There is a sphere in the eternal world which is called the Paradise of God. Within that sphere Jesus dwells with the disciples, and those who have been chosen to dwell there. This sphere is not the abode of the spirits or the angels; only those who have been solicited to dwell there can enter. Many there are who never come away to mingle with those who dwell in the other spheres. The grandeur and magnificence of this place is beyond conception, and those who dwell there have attained that spiritual enlightenment which enables them to understand all things pertaining to the divine in spiritual and human expression. A great many wonderful secrets are rent from the Paradise of God by spiritual vibration to the angelic and spiritual worlds, and after they have been understood by the members of the angelic world they are then given to the material world if it is ready to understand them.

The world is just beginning to understand that the spiritual ether which is above the earth's atmosphere abounds in the life force which emanates from the great universal God of heaven and earth, and that it is the substance of which the Creator is composed and cannot be destroyed; for it is spiritualized, etherealized electricity. Before it can enter into the form of a human being it has to be modified somewhat by contact with material forces, but all the same it is life. It is divine and emanates from God. It is the immortal principle of the Creator. It will be many years before this will be understood by the masses. It is something that must come gradually into the minds of the people, and like steps in progression one must be surmounted before the next one is understood. This divine principle to the spiritual sight is in the form of spiral vibrations and electrical cells. These two united form the perfect element of life. They are far too spiritual to be comprehended or seen as yet by the average mind. However, when the mind has developed itself sufficiently to comprehend spiritual principle, the creation of life will be from a higher standpoint than is embraced by the understanding of today.

The uniting of the spiral vibrations and electrical life cells forms the essence of immortal life, and since this is eternal from the Creator it cannot be destroyed, nor can it of itself waste its force. It may not be able to express itself in full strength through the physical expression, but that fault is with the material body, because the divine laws are not understood and because it is difficult to balance harmoniously material and spiritual elements. In the Paradise of God, divine laws are understood and harmony prevails, but these laws sent out to the angelic and spiritual mind and thence conveyed to material minds have not the power that they had in the beginning, for they have been lowered instead of elevated, being obliged to come through so many different elements.

If the soul would uplift itself at the time of the creation of life it would receive the divine light in its wonderful force, and the God principle would be expressed in the future growth in glorious spiritual development and unfoldment. I am sorry to say that the soul does not understand the higher laws of its being, and the life principle does not receive the divine insignia that it should nor that it was intended it should receive. The divine principle of life that emanates from God is continually at work. While in the physical body it really is the only force. The other principles which by some appear to be a part of the life-force, are only side tracks of one great course, and are nothing themselves if cut off from the one great course.

In analyzing the human system people forget to go beyond the body or the brain. They do not reach out to the divine principle which is the true force that keeps the machinery in working order. They never stop to think that there is a power outside of the physical body from which all of this wonderful activity emanates. The eye of the spiritual can behold the divine vibrations as they are directed toward the work of creation in human form. They are more powerful than any ray of electricity that has ever been seen by the material sight and are interesting to those who understand such divine forces.

In the Paradise of God all creative law has its source, and if there existed a human mind who could comprehend this the divine light would flow free and pure into the soul as it dwells within the human form. The laws of spiritual vibrations could be made more free and perfect if this were understood; there would not be so much inharmony, so much that is misunderstood existent upon the human plane of life, for the holy spirit of divine principle would be in harmony with the immortal soul. The human body would be a more fitting abiding place for the divine emanation from God, and the stamp of a higher force would be set upon the children of God.

The Children of God seems hardly appropriate when the expression is so imperfect as yet. We can only say "the children of men," for the God stamp upon their brows has not yet appeared. It is only within and has not expressed itself outwardly. Let us look forward to that time when every individual will bear upon his countenance the divine insignia of God. Let us pray that men will learn to look to the fountainhead of life and power and harmonize that knowledge with the God-principle existent within the soul. This will polarize the law of growth and reproduction and stamp the creation with the divine inheritance of immortal life. Then shall men be the children of God. Then shall the Paradise of God be attuned to the immortal and the divine within every created soul. Then shall all sin, sickness, poverty and ignorance be overcome and that which now appears evil shall develop into ultimate good. The divine kingdom within the soul may then be connected with the divine Kingdom of Heaven. By the law of spiritualized electrical vibrations, the divine essence of God, which vibrates through the spiritual ether above the earth's atmosphere, will then perform its true mission in connection with the children of men.

What a glorious world is that at the pinnacle of immortality, the Paradise of God—the Sphere of Divinity—where dwell the Saints of Light and where is the center of God-principle and power; where higher laws are created and made manifest, and sent by vibrations through the souls of angels to the subconscious mind of man. The Paradise of God is in beauty and grandeur beyond the comprehension of mortal man. Man must grow, unfold and develop gradually, and the time will come when the understanding of divinity will be to him as an open book.

God, the Creator and Giver of all life, is centered in the Paradise or sphere mentioned. From this great and glorious center of all light, life and wisdom divine force is generated through the heavenly and spiritual spheres and through all nature as it exists upon the material plane and the astral or solar system.

This is the divine principle of God and its supply is inexhaustible. As fast as it flows out and enters the soul of all nature it radiates back to the God-center and therefore cannot be destroyed. It is the highest and most spiritual force that can exist and is electrical in its nature, but so powerful and of such refined influence that it cannot be seen by the eye of the physical or comprehended by the mind of man. That some wonderful unseen force exists is well known, but to know what that force is man must be educated up to it by degrees. The spiritual mind can comprehend this principle, but not in its complete sense until it has unfolded and strengthened its powers of comprehension.

These vibrations as they emanate from the Godhead of life and power are of a deep purple or blue in tint, with a golden light upon each side. They penetrate the organism very strongly at a time when there is to be a parting of spiritual and material substance, also at the time of birth and creation. By this one may understand that the life force as it radiates through the physical is of God and is eternal with God; and the material plane, although so far removed from the sphere and center of divine life, is connected directly with this divine center mentioned. If this were not so, the material universe would be nothing at all. Chaos would be the result, for the supply that emanates from the sun could be cut off and there could be no life to exist in the world. Life is a chain of vibrations existing from the Godhead through the different forms of godly expression. *Since man himself is the direct principle of God, all other forms of godly expression have been created for the benefit of man and for his ultimate good, if he will only accept and use them according to divine law. If he does not do this, inharmony in his life is the result.*

The soul principle of every force in nature is generated first in the Paradise of God. These forces, as they are vibrated to material nature, take on a coarser material element in which they are clothed, just as the spirit of man is clothed in the material element of the body. The divine essence so refined in itself must have a coarser element to balance it when it has to do with material conditions upon the earth plane. Thought is composed of material and spiritual essence. Spiritual feeling has no material in it of itself, but has upon finding expression through the physical body. It is interesting to note the vibrations that connect with the divine in the Paradise of God as well as those vibrations which are more material in their nature and connect material minds with material. As I have said before, such things may be witnessed only by the highly spiritualized individual, and this power may be gained by inner reflection and concentration.

The different forces as they exist in God's Paradise are of many and wonderful colorings. The vibration that creates life in the individual is composed of twelve different colors, and each color relates to some force of the created organism in its spiritual and physical sense, and is worked out through the period of the individual's life.

The astro-spiritual organism is composed of electrical cells that draw their force from the great center of life. The storage battery of life and generative force is situated at the great nerve center, the Solar Plexus. The astro-spiritual is the spiritual connected with the physical, either while the body is in active use or while the spiritual is apart from the physical at night when the body is asleep. The physical organism of itself is magnetic and entirely dependent upon the spiritual for its life and supply, just as the spiritual is dependent upon the God principle for its supply. In the case of one, the force is intended to be eternal; while the other, according to the laws of the universe, must go back into nature. The particles that nature is continually taking up and throwing off have existed perhaps in different parts of the earth many miles distant. The scales of a fish may have been dissolved through chemical changes to exist in the deep red coloring of some person's lips, and so there is a force going on continually from the Paradise of God down to the working of life upon the earth plane.

The light which emanates from God's Paradise is of different forms and colors. A thought vibration is not of the same color as a life vibration for the reason that it does not require so many elements to build it up. A thought vibration is blue; a vibration of feeling is a blending of the two colors, rose-pink and green; a vibration sent out from the mind of the individual to benefit another financially is red in color; so one who would send out financial vibrations should hold that color in his mind when he is interested along this line.

He that overcometh shall inherit all things and I will be his God and he shall be my son.

                                          Revelations 21:7.

Ten

Spiritual Type of Jesus

It was in the eternal world, beyond the boundaries of the earth's atmosphere, a scene within one of the many beautiful spheres of Heaven. It was a summer scene, a background of grand old trees bending with the weight of fruit and blossoms. A group of angelic beings in white robes stood in the foreground, their attention fixed upon a grand, kingly figure surrounded by countless numbers of little children who were reclining upon the green grass, or floating just above in air and bending closely to the presence of the kingly figure who stood in the center of the group. It was the figure of a spiritual type of man. Tall and commanding in figure and clothed in a sparkling raiment of white, around which was a halo of spiritual light. The head was large with a profusion of brown, waving hair. The face was a study, such mighty strength was shown and yet such love and tenderness. The eyes were the most wonderful features of the face. They were of a dark purple color, and while their glance was filled with love and tenderness, yet there was a power that showed they could look right into the soul of an individual.

The light which was reflected from the person of this individual was so intense as to dazzle the eye at first glance. This manifestation being an indication of deep spirituality. This person, Jesus, had been talking to the angelic beings who surrounded him, and the words he had spoken had been received with intense interest. He had now finished his discourse and the little children had gathered around him to receive the spiritual vibrations of love sent out to them, and as he stood there an angel from a distance came, bringing to him a little child—a tiny little creature, so small that it seemed almost like a doll. He took it tenderly in his arms and touched its soft cheek and hair, and the face of the little one was uplifted to the face of Jesus as though it understood that here was love, gentleness and compassion. As he stood there holding the tiny infant, the group of angels separated and the figure of a woman was led in. As her eyes rested upon the face of Jesus they dropped, and the intense light dazzled her for a moment. Then a strange thing happened. She was forced to look straight at the face of Jesus, who held in his arms her little child; this child was the effect of her sin. The look directed toward her was so intense, so strange, and to her, so awful, for she knew that he read her soul, and for a moment such agony, such remorse, swept through her whole being that it seemed she suffered for a lifetime during that one moment. Then the figure of Jesus changed in its attitude and he took the little child and placed it in the mother's arms, lifting her from the ground, where she had fallen in her despair. For a moment his hands rested upon her head as though in blessing, and then, with her little child, she was led away to take up her life in one of the many spheres of the eternal world.

This is the Savior as I have seen him on the other side.

During December, 1901, when some parties were trying to make it appear that Jesus was only a historical myth, I asked my daughter to give me an article describing Jesus as she had seen him in Heaven, and this is it.

Eleven

A Trip to the Sun

Our party consists of my mother, an embodied spirit, my brother and myself, who are inhabitants of that Celestial Region beyond the shadows of the material plane. My brother and myself have visited that great world, the Sun, before, but it is the first time that our mother's spirit has ventured so far from the physical body.

It is night upon the earth, but to us there is no darkness. All is clear and bright and we float rapidly and easily through the air. There are no sensations of fear, only a delightful sense of freedom, that is quite unlike any material sensation. Up and up we go through the different gradations of atmosphere beyond the atmosphere of the earth, and we see the millions and millions of stars that hang in space, held in their place by the laws of attraction.

The air is filled with beings like ourselves, some of whom are embodied spirits and are connected by that long silver cord, which extends from the top of the head to the physical body now wrapped in sleep far away upon the earth plane.

Those who are disembodied have parted with that silver cord, and consequently there is no fear that they may be obliged to return to the earth on account of the restlessness of the sleeping body. What delightful scenes are shown all about us. And to our spiritual vision the sun in the distance looks like a great crimson globe, around which are different colored vibrations extending in all directions. These vibrations produce different effects by the time they pass through the various atmosphere extending between the earth and sun. The ether is quite different from the earth's atmosphere, since it contains elements too fine and ethereal to sustain the physical body.

As we draw near to the sun, we can see that the rays appear more powerful, although we feel no unpleasant effects, since heat has no effect upon the spiritual organism. Although the sun is many millions of miles away from the earth, we are enabled to reach it in a comparatively short space of time, and we find that its appearance is quite different from that shown to the people of the earth. In appearance it resembles burnished copper, and it has a hard, firm surface. The burning heat is in the interior and the rays sent off from the exterior are really generated from within. Upon some points of the sun are dark spots where the crust is quite thin and these are produced by extra heat upon the interior of these points. These are what are called "sunspots" and they produce much trouble upon the earth plane. Although this crust upon the sun is hard and firm to us and quite pleasant to walk upon, yet it would be impossible for physical beings to move about upon it, even though they could reach it, for it would be intensely hot to their feet.

The exterior of the sun is an interesting point, but we do not intend to stop here. We have the privilege and the power, as spiritual beings, to pass within, where greater wonders exist. It is comparatively easy to pass within the sun, and once within we find much to delight and inspire us. There are many wonderful caves and grottoes, where hang suspended pendants of every color in the rainbow. Of course the interior is not all alike. There are chambers in the sun, where are generated peculiar gases, that find their way eventually to the earth's atmosphere, having been changed and transmuted by chemical law into some element that is needed by the great world of nature. Some points within the sun were lakes of boiling fire, and the air was filled with showers of gold and silver rays. In some parts of the sun there were snow and ice, and when these sides were turned toward the earth there were generated cold vibrations, and the earth suffered from cold. The change in the seasons had much to do with this last fact.

In parts of the sun were summer scenes; there were lakes, rivers, mountains, flowers, trees, foliage and water. But in every part that we visited we found no inhabitants outside of those who had visited there for the purpose of exploration. In looking at the sun from the earth, one will often be able to distinguish dark spots. These sunspots are the exterior surface of a boiling, red-hot interior, and when they are in affinity with the earth there is intense heat. We saw much that was beautiful within the sun. In one magnificent grotto the place seemed bathed in a deep purple light, and curious formations resembling flowers, foliage and plants were seen. They appeared to be carved from iridescent stone, but upon examination proved to be the result of some gaseous disturbance within the depths of the grotto.

In one place far in the northwest corner of the sun was a point called the Fountain of Living Waters. A stream of water several hundred feet in diameter and of a deep, green color tossed its spray into the air. There was a peculiar power in this water and all who stood beneath it were conscious of a peculiar electric sensation vibrating through the spiritual body.

In some parts of the sun it would have been quite dark, had it not been for the spiritual power which enabled us to see light anywhere. One point particularly interesting was called the Arcana of Light. It was a point within the sun as large as the earth's surface, and was a center of the most brilliant light. Lights there were that had never been seen upon the material plane and most beautiful to look upon. There were parts where hung suspended upon the trees the most delicious appearing fruit, but it was only a formation and was not to eat. There were dark places that seemed like bottomless pits from whence were issuing white vapor and clouds of reddish light. These points are all serving a peculiar purpose designed by the Creator.

The different vibrations sent off by the sun were of various colors and power of strength. Some, by the time they reached the earth, contained but a very small part of the original element, others as they passed through the different gradations of atmosphere gathered to themselves various elements. These combined together formed an element that was very necessary to the sustainment and growth of physical nature. One vibration sent to the earth from the sun, unless cooled before reaching the earth plane, would scorch and consume everything in its path and total annihilation of the physical would be the result. The sun is composed of electric and magnetic force powerfully blended. We may say that the sun is the soul of the physical plane.

Twelve

A Trip Through Space

What a remarkable trip is that which takes one up through the material atmosphere beyond the spiritual ether, and still farther beyond the starry worlds made partially visible to the eye of material man! Millions of miles through space where new planetary systems are in a state of development for the years that are to come.

It is impossible for the mind of man to grasp the wonderful, brilliant kaleidoscopic picture that is shown to the spiritual being who is permitted to view God's handiwork, we may say, beyond the stars; meaning, of course, the stars which are visible to the inhabitants of the earth plane. But there are wonders that are still undreamed of.

Those beings who inhabit Mars and Venus have developed ingenuity enough to construct telescopes of sufficient power to bring the starry bodies beyond them within close range of their vision. In some respects the Martians are more ingenious than the inhabitants of the earth plane. They have a remarkable faculty in the making of glass—glass which cannot be broken and which is used largely in constructing their homes and in many other ways.

I have spoken of the people of Mars only in a way to serve as an illustration.

It is indeed interesting to behold what is taking place in the growth of the celestial bodies of space. In some regions of space beyond the boundaries of known stars we behold what we term star dust. There are regions of small stars in the process of formation; stars from the size of a silver dollar to those several miles in circumference. Such a shooting, hissing and roaring as goes on continually, if one were not a spiritual being I believe he would tremble for his life, had he the power to visit these regions of space that I have mentioned.

At times in these illimitable regions of space we seem to move through circles of intense light, yet there are no suns in close proximity. No stars either, for that matter; simply circle after circle of the most intense light—one might say a world of encircled lights—one within the other, sometimes of varied colors and tints, then again all of one color, flame color or pale gold.

In some regions of space we may travel for many miles through darkness and then suddenly come into a region where are softly falling rays of gold and silver light. In some places it will seem as though a terrific explosion is going on. Lightning plays and bombs of light seem to fly and break in all directions.

In these fiery regions dark intervening spaces are visible, but no feeling of fear is experienced, since all spiritual beings are able to comprehend that there is no celestial or terrestrial element which can harm them, so the experience of exploring space is more interesting and pleasant than otherwise.

The planets and stars visible to material eyes receive vibrations from the stars beyond them, just as the earth plane receives vibrations from the starry bodies above. These stars, as I have said, that are in the far beyond, are of different sizes and stages of development. Some hold one particular place, while others move in the region that I have been touching upon. Aerolites, comets and flying stars are exceedingly common. These lights of space never reach the earth, but other planetary systems receive the effect they produce, and the people who dwell upon the inhabited planets are frequently able to see them.

I will say here that it sometimes happens that a physical being in a cataleptic state will be able to send the spiritual body to these far regions of space, and the experience will be remembered after returning to the body, but such cases are extremely rare, as the physical is unable to stand the strain upon the electrical cord, which may suddenly snap, when all connection between the two ceases and death to the physical is the result. One may practice vacating his physical until the trip to regions beyond may be frequently accomplished with safety. It is a trip well worth remembering.

It is interesting to visit the starry bodies nearer the earth. There is the moon, with its peculiar phosphorescent light, its hollow mountains and terrific wind; also the planets Mars and Venus, that have become solidified and are inhabited by races of rather remarkable people. Then there is the planet Mercury, whose deep blue vibrations may be seen by the spiritual eye, affecting precious metals in the rocks, and causing them to grow and come forth. Then there is the fiery little planet of Neptune, where the elements are busily at work sending off peculiar atmospheric conditions that affect other planets as well as the earth.

There is a world of study in the planetary systems of space. Each separate star and planet has its own particular part to perform. There are some great planets that possess a light of their own; others have no light, but appear so, since they are surrounded by their satellites, which give them light. Other planets there are that receive their light from the sun the same as does the earth.

Frequently a starry planet will seem to twinkle rapidly, and not all minds are able to account for this. A planet with no light of its own, but surrounded by satellites, will seem to twinkle when in reality it is the smaller stars that encircle the larger ones that produce the twinkling effect witnessed by the people of the earth.

Part Two

CELESTION STUDY OF MAN

BY
Charles Samson
OF THE CELESTIAL SPHERES

What is man, that thou art mindful of him? and the son of man, that thou visiteth him?

DAVID.

One

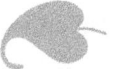

Nature of Man

Man is the masterpiece of God. No work has ever been created that compares with the marvelous mechanism of the human body or the surpassing beauty and power of the soul. Man little dreams of the wondrous possibilities folded within his soul. Few realize that man is free, that he has the power to make much or little of himself, and that he has this power according as he wills.

Man has three natures: material, mental and spiritual. His material nature pertains solely to his body. If this nature be in excess, he is not conscious of possessing a brain and soul. His appetites are low, like the animal; and his brain and soul remain as they are. There is no development or unfoldment. Man should not look down upon his material body, for it is the casket God has given him in which to hold the precious jewel, "the soul." He should therefore take good care of it, remembering that it is hard usage that wears it out and unfits it to longer contain the soul.

Man's second nature is the mental. It is that which thinks and plans. If this nature be in excess, the material body suffers, for the brain not only uses up its power but also draws upon the body and saps its strength. The brain itself is composed of millions and millions of little cells. These cells are replenished during sleep with the vital fluid, which is used up again during the work of the day. If a person continuously thinks upon one subject, he exhausts a certain part of the brain until it is no longer able to draw in the vital fluid. Softening of the brain is the result. There is between the brain and the spiritual part something that resembles a sheet of impression paper. It is, of course, of the same texture as the brain. The soul records its impressions upon this, making them clear to the brain, and the brain then gives them to the body. Some call this the conscious mind. It is the mind that man is conscious of.

There is another mind: the subconscious mind of the soul. If man would become complete master over himself he must find this mind. He can do so by frequently closing his eyes and going into the silence. In this way he can become conscious of the subconscious mind. Having knowledge of this, he can build up or restore any part of the human body. He can develop the muscles upon his arm by directing the power of his subconscious mind to that particular place. He may become his own physician. He may see the working of his brain and the blood coursing through the veins of his body. It is this mind that is with the soul, while the body is asleep and the spiritual form far away upon the astral plane. As yet its powers are undreamed of. The law of suggestion is frequently used by spirit friends upon the subconscious mind. Many people carry out the suggestions thus given them by their spirit friends, not knowing how and from whence they have been given.

What shall a man give in exchange for his soul?

JESUS

Two

Soul of Man

How marvelous is the work of God, displayed in the mechanism of the human body; how indescribably wonderful are the possibilities of the immortal soul, in their stages of unfoldment. In creating the human body God did a good work, but when he placed a divine soul within that body he did a greater work. To this he gave of his own principle and made all men sparks from the divine. The immortal principle of life he made to endure through all eternity.

Men should study themselves, in order to create harmony, peace, happiness and love in the world. In doing this, one can imagine that his body is like a mighty temple, and in order to come in touch with the God within, he must go daily into the temple and partake of the service therein. He must close his eyes and dream that he is passing into the Temple of Light. It will be difficult at first to get farther than the door, but he must persevere; presently the door opens, and he finds himself within a strange and wonderful place. Then come the winding corridors of the brain, with some new wonder in the thousands of rooms that are being continually rebuilt by the force which is ever working upon them.

Every thought that we think, like a little hammer, makes an impression upon the delicate walls of the brain-rooms. As we wander through these rooms we find those that are apparently unfinished; no impression seems to have reached them. These rooms are the latent possibilities of which man has no understanding. As he learns to enter daily into the temple, he begins to understand that he himself must develop these possibilities. He must find out himself just what can be accomplished by concentrated action upon the latent brain cells. The deeper he explores the more he finds.

The room of thought—what a wonderful place it is, what a busy place it is! Pictures are produced upon its walls. Some of these remain, others pass away almost as quickly as they are produced. There is the "Hall of Memory." The pictures that hang upon its walls represent all subjects. The artist that produces them is a master. He understands well the mixing of colors. His pictures are always bright. Many of them he would remove if he could do so, but it is impossible.

There are little printing presses in some of the rooms. These seem to be at work printing impressions that the mind may grasp and make clear to the physical body. In the brain of an inventor or mechanical genius we can find, as it were, pieces of machinery, bits of iron, screws and nails being fitted together; what a buzzing and whirling of wheels and belts there is, and what a power of sets the machinery in motion and keeps it a-going. We understand that the magnetic force is generated by the brain, while the electrical force is of the soul.

An examination of the outer surface of the brain shows that it consists of two parts, which are separated in the middle by a curtain. This may be compared to the structure of the

Tabernacle, described in the Bible, whose apartments are separated by a curtain. The part behind the curtain is the Holy of Holies. This is the place where man is supposed to enter if he would commune with God. It is a peculiar fact that this part of the brain is the seat of sensitive vibrations, and when it is active, man is in the most perfect state of harmony; he feels elevated and nearer to God than at any other time. Of course, this seat of sensitive vibrations does not of itself possess any power, but the soul-force is strongest and most highly developed at this point. This is pre-eminently the spiritual part of the Temple.

Three

Power of Thought

The brain is the printing press of the human body. It is a wonderful piece of mechanism. It prints its own and the soul's impression. The soul is the power behind the brain. This is the great life by which people "live, move and have their being. "The soul creates, the brain expresses." In the last lesson we talked about the brain-room of the "Temple of the Living God." After exploring its wonderful chambers, we come to another part of the temple, where there appears to be a wall separating us from what is within. We can surmount this only by practicing daily the power of concentration.

They who succeed in passing into this room find therein the key that solves the problem of existence. Herein are written the laws of God, making clear all secrets and mysteries. All who enter here may experience the peace that passeth understanding. The brain-room you thought was wonderful, but this one is far more so. Here you may watch a thought as it is first created. Here you may learn the secret of vibration—that marvelous electrical telegraph which sends its messages in the sixteenth part of a second. Here one may find harmony. Here he may have communion with his angel-friends. The part of man which is divine is located in this faraway corner of the Temple.

While sitting in one's room it is a good plan to try this exercise. Look at some object without thinking about it and close your eyes immediately. Do not think after closing your eyes. What do you see? The image of the object just looked at. This is gone in a second. This is the simplest form of an impression. It has no connection whatever with the brain-force. Close your eyes again and think of something. Now that thinking requires exertion; that is, you must use your brain-power to bring up the picture. This is a surface brain impression; that is, the picture is produced upon the outer surface of the brain. As the brain tissues are constantly changing from the old to the new, this impression is soon obliterated.

So far you have only been upon the surface. Now close your eyes again, and say to yourself, "I want to see what lies beyond this brain surface; this time I am going to use all my force to see what is there." Use your will as before and look within until you begin to see more clearly. Each time that you succeed makes you stronger and better prepared to see deeper. While you are practicing this, remember that all great writers, musicians, poets, artists and men remarkable for their ability as leaders of men have accomplished their work by retiring often within themselves. It was not easy for them at first, but by accustoming themselves to deep thought they became stronger and stronger, until the whole inner mechanism of their body and soul became clear to them.

Everybody has the power to enter into his conscious mind, because he has been taught to do so and has made himself familiar with it. Now this is not enough. He should become conscious of his subconscious mind. He can do this first by entering the conscious mind and then working his way to the mind of the soul. At first you may find that you can get no farther than your conscious mind, but don't give it up; keep on trying. Remember, you cannot reach the subconscious mind unless you first pass through the conscious mind. Perhaps you may try a week before seeing even a crevice that leads to the subconscious mind, and then suddenly you are amazed to find it all clear to you.

Having found your subconscious mind you can prepare to study it. A good way to come in touch with your inner mind is this: Close your eyes and try to think of something that made a lasting impression upon your life, something that had a deep feeling connected with it, either of joy or of grief. The picture you see is not upon your conscious mind. It has been produced upon your subconscious mind, the mind of your soul. Time cannot obliterate it. That impression will always remain. You will carry it with you into the next world. Your conscious mind, the mind of your brain, will perish with your body, but the other mind, the subconscious, is eternal.

The subconscious mind is very intellectual. It is capable of great power in its full development. It is the mind that accompanies the astral form in its travels through the night. If the astral form had not the power to leave the body, the person would walk in his sleep. It is during sleep that the subconscious mind predominates. Sleepwalkers are able to perform wonderful feats in climbing and walking in perilous places, because the subconscious mind dominates the physical.

Hark! 'Tis the voice of angels
 Borne in a song to me,
Over the field of glory,
 Over the jasper sea.

DOANE.

Four

Development of Soul Powers

When you enter the temple of your soul say to yourself, "May the peace of God, which passeth understanding, shed within me the light of knowledge and love divine. May it lift me up and show me the delights of the angelic world." This thought will help the soul to come into touch with God. It will enable it to unfold its powers, showing wonders undreamed of.

In this way one may find the key that unlocks all mystery. He can understand first how to pass into the brain, through the conscious mind to the temple of the soul, and from thence into the subconscious mind, and from thence transport his soul to any desired place, either upon the material plane or in the world beyond. Within the chamber of the subconscious mind, he will study thought-transference, vibration, inspiration, the secret of communion with the subconscious mind of all individuals, and the power of remembering distinctly the experiences that he had upon the astral plane during the hours of sleep.

By conquering and understanding one stage of development, a person will be prepared to understand the next stage, and so on, until finally he can say, I know that it is possible to solve the problem of existence upon the material plane and all others through the growth of strong powers of concentration and deep, earnest reflection. All life is a school. The material life and experience is a sort of preparatory institute for college in the life beyond, and you must learn each lesson as it comes. You cannot understand the teachings of college life until you have first mastered the problems of the preparatory school. So it is in the study of the human organism and the part which is divine.

Within the deep chambers of the soul are electric, vibratory wires that connect with the great nerve center of the body, the great "Solar Plexus." These little electric wires are like telegraphic lines which connect with the instrument of transmission. They are the wires that produce vibration, enabling two persons to come *en rapport* with one another, though they be thousands of miles apart. The more these wires are used the stronger they become and the greater is their power for good. They are continually sending out messages, but if the instrument at the other end is not *en rapport*, then the message reaches some individual for whom it was not intended.

The spiritual electricity in these little wires may take on a higher force by pure living, feeding the body on the most wholesome kind of food, and drinking pure water and plenty of it. Fruit is good, also fruit juices, as they are extracted in their pure state, are very good. If one would desire to develop his higher forces, well for him to carry salt upon his person.

Five

Wonders of the Inner Organism

New vistas of light and beauty are continually opening to the soul, that enters freely into the silence and there communes with the God of his spirit. All things are made clear to the newly awakened soul and "Heaven comes down to earth to greet." Angelic voices bring him their heaven-born messages, and he finds a pleasure in living that he never experienced before.

Pure thought, large aspiration, righteous living, and food of the purest quality, with the desire to understand the higher forces, may finally enable one to read the Commandments of God inscribed upon the tablet of his own soul. Understanding the inner power will enable one to commune telegraphically with others, as well as to see the vibrations that he sends out and where they strike.

All individuals reflect an aura of light from their personality. This aura can be discerned only by the spiritual sight. It is bright and its color brilliant in the degree that the person is spiritualized. If he possesses a moral weakness, it will be manifest in the spiritual aura. If his weakness is tobacco, dark brown spots will appear at intervals in his aura. If he loves the wine cup its symbol will be a scarlet flame. A highly spiritualized individual emits a light of very beautiful blue. This is the highest form of spiritual electricity.

There are many degrees of electricity, signifying different degrees of strength. The rose color signifies beautiful strength. It is not so penetrating, however, nor so potent as the white, blue or purple. The electricity that is visible to the physical eye is not spiritual but material electricity. Spiritual electricity is the higher form. The spiritual body is composed of this higher form of electricity. A strong and symmetrically developed physical body is magnetic. Such a body combined with a thoroughly electrified spiritual organization makes a strong and well-balanced individual.

Everyone should always bear in mind that his physical body is the casket which holds the "Pearl of Great Price," the "Jewel of God's Love," the Immortal Soul. He should always keep the "Temple of the Living God" pure and holy. By doing so he may worship therein in a more satisfactory manner than behind the walls of a church or anywhere else, for nothing is there that detracts from the Supreme Being whose presence is manifest at that sacred shrine, the "Holy of Holies."

That good and gentle man, Jesus Christ, was the most perfect embodiment of the divine principle. He was the manifestation of the Holy Ghost through the immortal soul. He was the most highly spiritualized being who understood the power from within. All men are the sons of God, but far below him in knowledge of divine truth and attainment of spirituality. He always dwelt in the light, the inner light of truth and divine reality.

The more one seeks for this inner light, the brighter and more penetrating it becomes, until finally it floods the whole temple of his being and reflects through the physical eye the glory from within. As one enters the silence he should say, "I desire the light; I wish it to flood my whole inner being and brighten up the farthest and darkest corner." He can grow strong by frequently desiring this power. In this way he will begin to see the most beautiful tints and colors, and then will come pictures and visions passing and repassing like the scenes of a panorama.

So much that is wonderful and beautiful may be developed through man's forces. Also many things that are very inharmonious and unpleasant may be produced in the same way. One's own thought vibration may cause sickness in his body or in the body of another. If a person thinks that he may take cold, he is liable to develop in a short time the symptoms of it. The explanation of this is the law of suggestion. This law of suggestion is frequently applied to the soul while the body is asleep. If a person is not in touch with the subconscious he will not remember any suggestion given him during sleep, but he will act out the suggestion while awake, not understanding why he does so. The more one studies the wonders of his organism, the more there is to learn.

There is no end to life; it is eternal, indestructible. The God principle which permeates all nature is continually renewing itself. As time goes on and man grows in knowledge, he becomes more capable of understanding the wonderful force by which life is created and truth unfolded. The great poet, Tennyson, said if he could only see what caused the seed to grow and how it developed its leaves and blossoms, he would then understand God. Knowing the powers of the seed and how the "spark of life" is derived from the Universal Whole, by which it carries out its plans—this knowledge is within the soul, but it, too, must be developed and unfolded. Tennyson would not say in this enlightened age that he did not think it possible to solve the mystery of the seed.

Six

Significance of Color Vibrations

Happy is he who realizes the wonders of his own organism. Happy is he who knows that he is endowed with beneficent senses, which require only an awakening from their dormant state to make the world a more habitable and beautiful place to live in. If a person aspires to be a teacher, he himself must first acquire the desired knowledge and show himself capable of imparting it to others. He must be master of himself. He will then be able to conquer all things. Each new step that he takes will reveal to him more beauty, more grandeur and greater possibilities.

What could be more desirable than to behold with closed eyes the inner workings of nature—to see that printing press of the human brain, working with greater rapidity than any machine in a newspaper office, and sending out vibrations through the electric wires that ran through the body to the great nerve center, The Solar Plexus; to see the electric vibrations passing out of the physical body in all directions and to all points of the universe; to see the thoughts that are sent to the mind, to some of them striking unresponsive centers and bounding off to other receptive minds for which they were not intended; and then to see the grand spiritual aura which shows the events that are to come into the individual's life in the future. What could one see that would be more desirable than all this?

These wonders just mentioned and many more like them make a most fascinating study to the soul in the process of unfoldment. The order in which we may study these truths is as follows: Materialism and the Body, Menthology and the Brain, Spiritual Embodiment or the Soul in the Body, Astrae or the Study of the Soul on the Astral Plane, Spiritualism or Disembodiment pertaining to life in the Spirit World, Celestialism or the Study of an Angel or developed spirit and the laws which govern the Celestial World.

In the cure of disease, knowledge of color vibrations is most important. It is one that should be well analyzed. In treating disease by mind power, one should send out vibrations of certain colors for certain maladies. A person suffering from lung trouble should receive red vibrations followed by blue. These two will exert an influence that is more healing than any of the others. In treating those who suffer from heart trouble one should use the seven primary colors, since the heart is the main organ of the physical body. Healing power may be exerted by placing colored glass in the region of an afflicted part and allowing the light from a candle, electric bulb, or lamp to shine directly one it. Colored electric bulbs, placed before diseased parts, are helpful.

There are people who should have particular colors about them, as they draw certain influences that are either helpful or detrimental. Black is not a helpful color; it draws depressing influences. The mourner who wears black will be unhappy for a much longer period than she would be by discarding the black, and wearing a color pleasanter to the sight and calculated to suggest bright and happy thoughts. A person having a sympathetic temperament should never wear red. Blue is the principal color for them to wear, as it is the negative element in opposition to the abundance of warm, red, positive blood that courses through the veins. A cold-blooded, negative person should always have about them warm, bright colors, for these will help them supply the force that they lack. Everyone should wear upon their person their particular color. It is not necessary that it be worn where it is visible at all times, but it is well for them to think of their particular color frequently, as it will be helpful to them.

All the forces of nature have different color vibrations. These vibrations can be seen only by the spiritual eye. Those who have laid aside the body and others that have learned while upon the material plane to solve the problem of existence for themselves—these can see the color vibrations of nature. Musical tones have color vibrations. Each tone produced upon the piano has its own peculiar color vibration. The minor tones have soft, delicately-tinted vibrations, while the opposite colors are produced by the higher tones. These are interesting truths in themselves, and should be thoroughly studied and well understood.

Seven

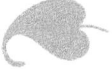

Dualistic Forces Harmonized

In material strength man is a superb animal, in spiritual power he is a divine masterpiece. In his material and spiritual strength he is a creator, the embodiment and expression of the divine principle. Pope said, "All are but parts of one stupendous whole, whose body nature is, and God the soul."

With an understanding of the spiritual and physical bodies will come the solution of deeper and higher problems. With an understanding of the dual-man will come the ability to interpret aright the teachings of the God-head in nature. Jesus' death upon the cross will no longer mean that he was crucified to save the souls of men. Every man must work out his own salvation. Jesus came as an example to show men how to live. The fact that he was crucified by men will no longer be construed as the working out of a divine law. There was not "one jot or tittle" of the principle of divine law in it. It was a most inhuman act.

Through a knowledge of the teachings of "Celestion," man can prove himself the Son of God and make for himself a heaven, though still an inhabitant on the material plane. The solution of the great problems of Labor and Reform will be to him as an open book. He will understand that great financial problems can be worked out by the law of Universal Brotherhood. The laboring man and the capitalist are each dependent upon the other for existence on the earth plane. When this fact becomes universally known, men will strive to help others as they have never done. The world's ideas and understanding of things spiritual will be enlarged. The horizon of thought and action will indeed be broadened. There will be wonderful inventions on land and sea. People will be enabled to reach distant lands in the time that it now takes to travel a hundred miles.

Man is still in his infancy as regards great possibilities. The physical eyes are the outer windows of the soul. These as we know are marvelous pieces of mechanism, but they are not so wonderfully constructed as are the inner windows of the spiritual organism. It is through these physical eyes or windows of the soul that a great deal of the inner-force finds expression. One may understand a considerable about the organs of sight by studying the camera and its lens. When one looks at an object it is focused upon the retina of the eye. If conditions are good the object is photographed upon the inner plate and will remain a definite or indefinite period. Some objects require the developing process to fix them. That process is feeling.

Feeling has two forces, one producing pleasant experiences and the other causing grief, remorse or sorrow. Anything that is produced by either of these forces will endure forever. Time cannot obliterate the effects produced. These are interesting facts, that every man should prove to his own satisfaction, and which he may do by frequently making a thorough examination of himself.

Strong Son of God, Immortal Love,
    Whom we, that have not seen thy face,
By faith, and faith alone embrace,
    Believe in where we cannot prove.

                                          TENNYSON.

Eight

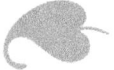

Physical and Psychical Non-Transmutable

Man is dual, the inhabitant of two bodies—physical and divine. The forces that build up his two bodies consist of entirely different elements. It is impossible to transmute the force of the physical into that of the spiritual. That which composes the physical can be disintegrated and used in other physical expressions. That which builds up the spiritual is from God. This building is his completed work, good and perfect, but the physical body is imperfect.

The statement that Christ laid in the tomb three days and then arose from the dead should not be taken in a literal sense. While he did lay in the tomb, it was in a trance or cataleptic state. His spiritual body which was in Heaven was still connected with the physical by the electric force that holds body and spirit together. He was to all appearance dead, but not so in reality. When his spirit ascended to Heaven to dwell there, it was his immortal body that was taken up, for does not the

Bible say, "Flesh and blood cannot inherit the Kingdom of Heaven"? There has been a mistake in the translation of the part where reference is made to the disappearance of his body and the ascension of the physical; these things did not occur. When Jesus showed his side with the wounds in it he took on the physical from the elements of nature in order to make himself visible to his friends. This is done in the materialization of forms at séances and in producing phantasms upon photographs and in other ways.

At a séance where spirits are to be materialized, there must be present a spiritual chemist, who understands thoroughly the laws and forces of chemistry. This chemist finds the air filled with elements that go to build up physical; also, he takes by the law of attraction particles from the physical beings who are present. He holds out his hands and sends out to the person whom he wishes to draw from electric vibrations. The spiritual form stands directly in front of him and as the elements are disintegrated from the physical they form about the spiritual. It will not do to take very much from the physical being, as it would weaken him too much, and so in order to complete the building up of the form, particles are taken from the atmosphere. When the greater part of the materialized form is built up from the elements of the atmosphere, it remains only for a moment and then goes to pieces. When there are a number of people present to draw from who are strong physically, then the body remains visible a greater length of time than the other way.

When you look at a sunbeam that slants across the room, you will see that it is filled with minute particles that move constantly. It is upon such particles that the spiritual chemist sends out electrical vibrations, and by this force they are brought up and united around the spiritual body to make it visible. There are different ways of producing materialization. Sometimes the entire physical form of the medium is disintegrated or taken built up so as to resemble the spirit, who occupies the physical body that has just been changed. In such a case, a tall blonde woman would appear as a short, dark spirit in materialized form. Since the spirits themselves build themselves up in the form of the medium, there is no reason to speak of it as fraud. As was said, this is done by the spirit-chemist, who holds out his hands and sends forth vibrations at the command of his thought, and wherever these vibrations strike there is a drawing of the elements toward the spiritual form that is being built up. Thought must be used at the same time. The chemist must think of what he is going to do, and that thought-force draws the elements together, which the physical is constantly throwing off.

When spirits take flowers from different parts of the universe they disintegrate them; that is, they remove by the law of chemical action the spiritual element of the flower from the physical. They take this spiritual element where the flowers are to be materialized, and then they gather together the material elements from the atmosphere and build them up around it, and immediately the room is filled with flowers. Where they came from is a mystery to those present. If a person wishes to send his spiritual form out of his body to be made visible to his friends, a great deal of practice is required to do this. It is easy enough to send the spiritual body out of the physical, but not so easy to make it visible to his friends; for the spiritual form must also take on the physical elements, if it is to be made manifest.

The one who wishes to transport himself out of his body must think very intently upon the most spiritual thing that he can bring to mind, and become so absorbed in his thought that nothing material appears to reach him. In a few moments he loses himself as it were, and then he will soon be out of his body. He can without effort visit his friends, and if he wishes to show himself to them he must use his electrical force to draw around him the material elements of nature. The man who wishes to disintegrate his body at the time of death must do so before he arises into the air. Flesh, blood and bones are too heavy to move through the air; they must be dissolved by chemical action before they can become a part of the atmosphere.

Why should a person care for his physical body after the spirit has left it? According to the divine plan, death is a natural law, and no living person can work successfully against God's law. The particles which constitute the physical body belong to the atmosphere and must return to the atmosphere, but the body must be dissolved and changed by the forces of nature. A person should care for the physical while it holds the spiritual. He should keep it in perfect health. When the connection between the two no longer exists, then the material work of the individual has ended, his soul can no longer dwell within the body, and the body must again become a part of nature.

All persons who are interested in the study of divine philosophy should take up the study of chemistry. By doing this he will accomplish a great deal that they could not do otherwise. They cannot do away with the philosophy of things. That is impossible. Things that are merely practical are robbed of their beauty. Practical facts clothed in philosophy must be accepted.

Nine

Soul Progressive, Not Retrogressive

Scientists and men of intellectual power believe that man undergoes a complete change once in seven years. The fact is that the physical man changes daily. But the spiritual form existent within the physical structure does not change; that is, it does not take on any different substance from that with which it was created. It is a part of the Divine, but not of as high an order as it will be later on, as it passes through different periods of progression, being continually drawn nearer to the God-head or Center of all life.

In passing through the different centers of transfiguration the spiritual form becomes each time more ethereal and beautiful. But it never loses its identity or individuality. One may become more spiritual and beautiful, and yet there is always something about him that belongs distinctly to himself, and which one may see. The spiritual form, as it passes through the first center of life, is electrical. The force which is generated from it is electrical. It is this form of spiritual substance that is best known to the physical. But the force surrounding it is not so high as that in the center above, since as one continues to pass onward he draws nearer to the God-center. The force that prevails in the second center of life is Argaon.[1]

They who pass through it take on a higher state of being; that is, more beautiful and ethereal.

A created soul is made in the divine image. It cannot go into a lower form than it is, because it is the highest conception or expression of the Creator. You may say it is the Masterpiece of God and is good of itself and capable of mighty unfoldment. There are various reasons to account for the fact that it seems to some people that they have been reincarnated. The thoughts of the mother while carrying her child in embryo will become sometimes so impressed upon the plastic mind as to be indelibly printed there, and as the child grows in material life and becomes old enough to reflect and analyze itself, it seems conscious that it was once some other person or lived in some other form. I will give an example.

A family living years ago in an Eastern state had among its members a beautiful little child of five years. It was a very precocious child. It passed away when almost six years of age. Its name was Carrie. About six months after its death another child was born into the family. This child was christened Mary. The mother had grieved continually and thought daily about the child that had passed away, and hoped that the one who was soon to be born would be like her little Carrie. Just as soon as the child Mary could talk she persisted in saying that her name was "Carrie," not Mary, and as she grew older she showed many traits that were identical with those of the departed child. This was a case of pre-natal influence. But the

---

[1] Argaon[Argon]: This means a higher form of atmosphere.

Reincarnationist would say that the child was a reincarnation of the one who had passed on some months before her birth. This shows that things are not always what they appear to be.

Celestion teachings show that in this day man has grown toward a higher understanding than that of years long ago passed. The soul, the man himself, is the highest expression of God; if he commits a crime and creates inharmony, it is he himself that is to be called to account, not his Creator. Much of the evil in the world is the result of ignorance. The time is not far distant when he will be ashamed to be ignorant. *We believe that evil is committed through the desire to satisfy some demand of the physical body, not the soul.* Conscience is in the soul, and many a man who has committed the foulest of crimes has been tormented day and night by the pangs of conscience. We cannot believe, therefore, that it is the soul which is wrong, but that at the time of committing the sin man's lower nature prevailed and would not listen to the promptings of the soul.

A soul that has long dwelt in a perverted body may finally despair of trying to reform the individual himself, and consequently become contaminated. After passing over it may retain for a time the evil tendencies and desires, but certainly not for long, as it cannot commit crime in the Spirit World. There every man is known as he is, and if he would do wrong he must come to the earth plane to do it. There is but little satisfaction in this, however, and the contaminated soul soon wearies of it, and desires progression and to be able to reap the rewards of those who are spiritual in life and nature. In coming into contact with his victim upon the other side, the remorse of conscience for a murderer is most intense. It is also for those who have wronged individuals in earth life when they meet them in the Spirit World, where every wrong committed in the previous life is known. It is indeed a wonderful plan by which the soul may grow out of darkness into light and through its own efforts become a bright and shining light in the Spirit World.

The life-cells existent within the physical organism hold within themselves the microscopic germs of future life. They are so infinitesimal that their existence is known only from the spiritual understanding. The great problem of life and existence is still agitating the world. What is life? From whence does it come? Does it have a beginning and end? I say that the individual has within him this day the microscopic principle of being that will exist thousands of years from now, and that beings who existed thousands of years in the past had within their own organisms the embryonic forces that are active within man today. In that way life grows and it is impossible to trace its beginning, and it has no ending, for life is eternal. There is no record in the Spirit World that a soul has ever perished. The Creator of the Universe is all-powerful and neverending. The God principle quickens individual life, causing it to grow and expand. The soul itself is of God, but the physical which grows from the spiritual is of man's own creation. God has given to man the power to create; but the Divine Center, the Ego of Life, is from God and is perfect. The physical imperfect.

At the time of creation divine vibrations from the God-center come in contact with the life-germ and quicken it into action. Hitherto it was existent but dormant; with the quickening process it becomes suddenly awakened and begins to grow and expand. You may say there is no period when life really begins. It may not be perceptible on account of its microscopic appearance, or it not be made conscious, though in so small a form that no eye save that of the Creator may see it. The very air is filled with force that must be taken into the physical in order to make it grow and to sustain it, but the soul principle, the divine center, draws its supply from the God-head, higher up. There is no drain upon this principle, for it is eternal and vibrates from God himself. The physical must work in order to sustain itself, but the spiritual is kept up by the higher power. The spiritual gives power also to the physical so long as the physical helps to sustain itself.

Spiritual beings do not accept Reincarnation. Man, "the Masterpiece of God," has within him the power to expand and go forward instead of backward. Man may find within nature many symbols by which he can learn how to guide himself. A tree is always a tree; it never goes back into any other form of nature. The same is true of all forms of nature; they perpetuate their own species. As the flower is the soul of the seed, so a spiritual being is the higher part of the physical. Nature is progressive, not retrogressive. It goes forward, instead of backward. This is one of the beauties of God's law. According to the spiritual idea Karma[2] is the life-center from whence vibrate the principles that communicate or connect with the soul. This supply is inexhaustible; it cannot be destroyed; it is all good, and he who receives from that Karmic-center cannot move backward. He must either remain as he is or move forward along the scale of progression. *Karma in spirit is God; in the physical it is the individual himself with his individuality, his consciousness and his higher faculties.*

There is more in the Spiritualistic idea of Karma than there is in the Theosophical. To us it is the more satisfying and the more rational. We like to understand that our individuality cannot be destroyed and that we are the highest expression

---

[2] Karma—Spiritual beings give a higher meaning to Karma than the Theosophical definition. They believe and understand it to be the Life-force which vibrates with the soul.

of God. If he has created within us the principles that are to lead us to a higher growth, would it be reasonable, think you, to stifle them by causing the immortal soul to dwell in some lower form of life. The soul of man is a mighty flame from the divine Center, while that of an animal is but a spark and is on a lower scale than humanity. It is pleasant to think that the soul of man may go on perfecting itself through all eternity, and always retain its own personality, that which is high and yet peculiar to itself. It should make us happy to realize this.

We, spiritual beings, like to think of the Creator as one who is all-loving, all-wise and all-powerful; that he is infinitely above all weakness, above a sin that may be in the physical nature. We cannot ascribe to him hate, inconsistency, wrath, cruelty or inharmony. We can only credit him with good and to him we must look for goodness, love and higher wisdom.

Ten

Immortality of the Soul

There has been much discussion regarding the possibility of death to the soul upon the higher side of life. The truth is this. The physical body is nothing of itself. It is the principle of life that gives activity to the physical body. When this principle leaves the body it takes up a higher existence on the other side of life. This principle is part of the Creator and emanates from him. It is life in its purest and highest form. Its nature is electrical and composed of electrical cells stored with vital power. The physical body is magnetic and of an entirely different principle. The physical body is a manifestation of the spiritual, but it is not immortal as is the case of the spiritual.

There is no record in the spiritual world of a soul ever having perished. They who have existed for thousands of years on the other side of life furnish evidence of this fact. Families are living together who have been united for many a year. If death were possible to the soul, these family ties would have been broken in some cases at least.

In the spiritual world we are instructed by philosophers and teachers that the soul is immortal, that it cannot die, since it belongs to God and his eternal principle. The Bible says: "The soul that sinneth, it shall die." This is explained as follows: The word soul is sometimes used in speaking of an individual and does not especially refer to the life principle. "The soul that sinneth," that is, it shall not grow; it shall remain dormant and asleep within the physical body. Sleep may be likened unto death by the physical mind. There is not sufficient explanation in the different parts of the Bible to make the meaning clear. Many passages are therefore written in symbols to be translated by the thoughtful mind.

In all godly creations there is an eternal principle of life. You may take the seed and keep it for years; then plant it and the life is shown in the green shaft which springs up through the ground. Nature renews itself year after year, showing that life in nature is immortal, and since man is the highest manifestation of God, how inconsistent it would be to believe that God's masterpiece would not be endowed with immortal life! When the physical body has lost its life force, one may insert a needle into the flesh and the puncture remains open. In a trance condition, when the body is to all appearance dead, the same experiment may be tried and the puncture will close up.

The foregoing fact proves that while the body is the same in its component parts, something is gone. If the body itself is all there is and it is an independent force of itself, why can it not restore itself and do the same as before? This proves that the physical body is not independent of itself. It is the servant of the spirit. The spiritual principle is independent, because it is from God. It requires no renewal, but is created for eternity.

He would be a strange Creator who gives to the soul grand and noble ambitions, the gift of genius and talent, the faculty of love, if these were to be all annihilated and cease to exist with the destruction of the soul and all its beautiful qualities.

The atmosphere is aglow with life force that is not visible to the physical sight. A flower is immortal. When it fades the spiritual form of the flower takes up its existence in the atmosphere, while the material principle takes its place in the building up of the physical.

People say that a child has not life until the quickening. This is not so. There is life from the very beginning, but it is not always apparent, through the limitations of the physical mind. Real life of itself cannot be destroyed. There is no created element that may destroy it. People should understand that a separation of forces does not mean the destruction of life in itself. Heat and cold, light and darkness are the physical manifestations of God, and have no effect upon the spiritual expression, the immortal soul.

As I have said, the spiritual form, while it resembles the physical, has in place of organs of digestion, vibratory life cells, connecting with a mighty center of force, whose supply may never diminish. This body of vibrating life cells is created for eternity. The immortal body is much more beautiful than the physical, for it possesses no defects, no parts that are inharmonious. All is well balanced in the spiritual, for the spiritual is in touch with divine life and cannot be otherwise than perfect in construction. It is a beautiful thought to realize that there can exist no crippled, deformed bodies, no sightless eyes, no defective sense of hearing, no inharmony of any kind in the eternal world. Life of itself is beautiful, and how necessary that its manifestation be beautiful instead of unpleasant.

The Creator has given to man the power to create beauty if he will. It seems from the sights one sees in the public walks of life, that man preferred to create ugliness instead of beauty. Beauty is of God, ugliness is of man. God has many ways of expressing himself. Nature is God materialized. His divine spark radiates all through nature. The law of production, growth and renewal is all of God. That which seems like death is only chemical action upon the different forces that are united in the building up of form.

If one will watch a sunbeam as it slants across a room he will notice tiny particles that seem to be continually moving. These particles are atoms that have been changed by the chemicalization of nature to be taken into the physical organism or into the plant life and then to be sent out again, as life is an endless round of renewal and separation.

The existing soul, through all the periods of its growth, holds within itself mighty faculties of embryonic form. One may find an illustration of my meaning by taking a lilac twig in midwinter and removing the little brown covering at the top of the twig. Removing this covering, one finds the tiny green leaves curled about a small bunch of green buds so small that they can scarcely be seen with the naked eye. The possibilities of this tiny bunch of green are not apparent as yet. It is the soul of the plant, however, and in it the thoughtful mind may find an illustration of the soul's development, growth unfoldment.

The spark of immortality which emanates from God has the faculties within it in miniature form. The life force within, which cannot perish, will express itself through the rounding out of the beautiful faculties which God has planted in embryonic form in the heart of every soul-cell.

The soul, be it ever so small, is a miniature of perfection complete in itself, according to divine law. Its law is growth in fullness and beauty. The physical expression of the soul may not equal in strength and beauty the mighty force which gave it life and caused it to grow and unfold, for one is the cause and the other the effect.

The soul, as it grows and unfolds within the physical body, finds a time when it demands something higher and better than the outward covering and so, like the soul of the worm (the gorgeous butterfly), it bursts its shackles and soars onward toward immortality—Immortality, that glorious inheritance that the Creator has left for his children to win.

People have said that one particular region in the physical body must be the seat of the soul. We who know say that the soul generates itself through every part of the physical body. Wherever there is sensation there is soul. Every nerve cell of the physical body has an electric filament running through it that is of soul-force. When life ceases to exist in a particular part, it does not follow that the life force is dead. On account of the failure of the physical, the life-force cannot express itself to the physical, even though it exist the same as before. It is because the physical understanding is so dense that it cannot comprehend the spiritual.

The tip ends of the fingers have brain and soul-force, but this force is dormant unless exercised and developed. One can do wonderful things through the exercise of these functions if he will. He can learn to distinguish colors in the dark and handle an article and give its complete history. Many blind people have developed this faculty and used it to supply the deficient power of physical sight.

People have wondered why the right hand possesses so much more power than the left. The answer is very simple. It is because the left is not used as much as the right. Children should be taught to use both hands. The result will be equal strength on both sides. If people used only one leg in walking, the corresponding leg would be deficient in strength.

It is a well known fact that the left half of the brain controls the right side and vice versa. One side of the brain is positive, the other negative, and these two forces must be balanced before power will result. Therefore, if the left side of the brain is positive, the right side is negative. The two forces united give that mighty strength expressed through the physical. To be sure, the soul has its centers of force in the physical body, and the supply cut off from any of these centers results in death to the physical.

The electrical vibrations of the soul which radiate through the different parts of the physical are, after death, united in one grand force in the spiritual body.

A vibration is an electric or magnetic current which, when sent to any particular point, produces and expression or impression. One may see a vibration by looking at an electric arc light at night. Of course, the vibrations of the spiritual force are of a higher order than those of an electric light, but one may find an illustration in them if he will study them. The vibrations of the spiritual are electrical, while those of the physical are magnetic. Electrical force is immortal; magnetic force is perishable and must be continually renewed. These two forces vary in form and color. One is irregular in form and of a deep purple, radiating, golden tinge;

the other is expressed in a straight line and is rose pink in color.

A person who possesses an intense vitality will radiate the magnetic vibrations. One who is very spiritual and soulful in his nature will send out the electrical vibrations.

Magna is health; electra is spirit. One who is balanced in these two forces is a power in himself. The gentle Jesus was perfectly balanced in his magnetic and electrical strength, and so his life was a power within itself.

The electrical vibrations of the spiritual are connected at the brain, the heart and the solar plexus. This is the reason why these different points are vital centers, and if the supply is cut off death ensues to the body. These truths of which I have spoken pertain to the immortality of the soul. While it is an inmate of the physical, its higher form of expression shows it to be independent entirely of the physical, growing, developing and unfolding in the higher life, which has no limitations; and where it may come into the complete fullness of the power for which it has been created. This is the fulfilling of the law that the soul is a part of that one great whole whose body nature is and God the whole.

Jerusalem! Jerusalem!
 Thy streets of pearl and gold
Are trod by the blest feet of them
 We knew and loved of old.
Their voices full of calm delight
 Steal through the radiant air—
Jerusalem! Jerusalem!
 Our hearts are with them there.

Anonymous.

Eleven

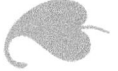

Communications on the Heavenly Life

Strange and wonderful events transpire daily in that region beyond the earth's atmosphere known as the Spirit World. Few there are who can form any conception of that life who have not looked upon its transcendent grandeur and spiritual beauty.

We may say that the higher world does not occupy space, for in the spiritual sense there is no limit to space; there is no top, no bottom, no height or depth. That which appears to the physical sight to be a boundary line between the earth and the sky is nothing more nor less than an effect.

The reality of life and condition is found in the eternal world. People upon the physical plane are walking about half of the time in a dream or dazed condition. They do not experience the reality of life that is to be found in the higher world. In the eternal world there is plenty of room for millions and millions of souls who are yet to come, and yet all places there are built up and are open to the visitation of the Angelic Host.

It is difficult for the material mind to realize how one million spirits can occupy a very small space and yet be of average height and form. It is true, nevertheless, and is one of those realities that must be seen to be understood. The mind and eye of the spirit possess qualifications that are above those of the physical. The spiritual eye can see all parts of the physical body, internally and externally. It is impossible for the physical eye to see the back of the head unless it is reflected in a mirror, but the spiritual eye can see the back of the head and all that is going on in the distance from the rear. I only mention this as a curious but nevertheless true fact.

Religion in the eternal world is of the highest standard. There is but one religion, and that is a beautiful one. It accepts all souls and is the religion of God. It teaches of progression for all men and universal opportunity for those who take on the garment of immortality. Love is the law upon which the religion of Heaven is based. The love of God for His children, even though they err, for all may be purified through divine love.

Young children of the higher world are taught at a very tender age to become lecturers and speakers, and there are chapels and lecture halls in that world where the speakers and members of the choir are all young children. The remarks they make and the thoughts given out would do credit to many a man of intellect. This is one of the beautiful teachings of the higher life, for in that world where people desire progression and intellectual growth speakers are essential, and the little child who is taught to give voice to his thoughts will in later years be able to touch the souls of the multitude with his inspired thought and his wonderful teachings.

The gentle Christ who walks about among the people produces in the minds of the young children a desire to follow in his footsteps, for all who are brought in contact with that lovable personality are filled with a strange and wonderful peace, which is the peace that cannot be found in the physical.

The religion of heaven is based upon understanding, not faith, and may be analyzed and reasoned out to the complete satisfaction of all who enter that life. The light which emanates from the divine finds its way into all souls and they can but say "It is well. Before I saw through a glass darkly, but now all truths have been revealed unto me, and I rejoice in the fact that all laws are carried out through the divine plan." New ideas, new thoughts are being continually worked out in the higher world, but there is a great deal for which the people of the earth are not ready. Certain inventions that are about to be given to the world have been known in the spirit life for twenty-five years, and many of the ideas that I have given out through my writing will be more favorably received a year from now than they are at the present time.

The mind of man is going through the crucible to make it ready for the grand and beautiful touch of the divine hand.

There is a building in the celestial world called the Temple of God. This building extends for several miles and is being continually filled with the creations of God. This building is consecrated to God. No angel's work may enter here, only that which pertains to God. *What a marvelous creation is this Temple with God's workmanship displayed upon every hand.* Upon the walls of this Temple may be seen moving pictures that seem endowed with life scenes, many of them are scenes that are transpiring in God's Kingdom of the higher sphere. These marvelous pictures must be seen to be comprehended, for they are beyond power of description. This Temple is always flooded with a light in which is blended fifteen different colors that vibrate in different forms. At times these lights seem to arrange themselves in the form of beautiful flowers; then again they appear to be straight or horizontal lines with all colors shaded in the most artistic arrangement. Then again these lights will roll like billowy clouds in the most intense brilliancy of coloring and the softest, most delicate tints imaginable. This is divine light, and the soul that draws near to such light appears suddenly glorified. He surely is in touch with the divine who can draw near to this wonderful form of light. At times the place will seem to be filled with millions and millions of stars of many colors, the different forms of light being symbols of some force that is about to be carried out upon the earth. The symbol of stars meaning that new discoveries and wonderful inventions are about to occur on the earth. Golden lights and stars refer to the fact that indications pertaining to discoveries and powers of gold are working their way upon the earth. Certain colors, waves and forms show revelations of a spiritual nature of the rocks, the sea or the air. The individual well versed in spiritual law can enter the Temple of God and be able to tell the meaning of the varied tints, stripes, spheres, zig-zag or horizontal lines, or different colored stars.

There are a few people upon the earth who have the gift of seeing with their own eyes the things that I have described that take place in the Temple of God. How beautiful it is to gaze at a small purple spot and see it suddenly open out, showing a basket of beautiful flowers or a fountain throwing up sprays of rainbow-tinted water; or again to see the whole interior of the room festooned with bowknots of the most beautiful flowers and shining over all the strange and beautiful light that I have described upon a previous page. How wonderful and beautiful it all is, the glorious and beautiful Temple wherein are displayed the wonderful creations of the divine. My soul is filled with delight as I reflect upon the wonders of thy creation. I can only say in the name of the Divine, "It is well."

Twelve

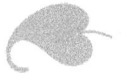

Books and Their Writers

Those who were writers in earth life are at work in the eternal world upon a higher line of thought than they wrote while on earth. T. H. Burgoyne, who gave to the world his work entitled "The Light of Egypt," has produced upon the other side a strangely fascinating work written under the title of "The Light of Eternity." This work corrects many of the errors of his former work and goes to show that things are not what they seem when viewed through the light of the material mind. In this work the higher spiritual laws are set forth and a great deal is shown that may be accomplished by the power of thought in its higher development.

The books and literature of Heaven are largely produced by the expression of thought upon the open page. One has only to think and immediately the words appear in indelible lettering. A person may understand by this that a very lofty development of the thought power must be acquired to produce such an expression as I have mentioned.

In the production of spiritual books, thought has passed through the development stage to one of spiritual unfoldment. The expressions are imprinted upon large sheets of different tints and colors. These sheets are made from the spiritual flowers pressed out although they contain the expressed thoughts, they may be said to be alive, for you cannot destroy the eternal life-principle in a spiritual flower, no matter into what form you fold or press it.

"The Light of Eternity" serves as a book of instruction for those who would progress in the higher philosophy of spiritual truth, and for those in different stages of development as well. There are many thoughts produced upon its pages that cannot be understood by those who have not attained a very high stage of unfoldment. Among some things written in the book is this: *"The immutable laws of God radiate through all forms of nature, both spiritual and material. And it would be an utter impossibility for any man to withdraw himself from God, for God is everywhere."* The divine spark has found expression within every immortal soul. When I say every immortal soul, I mean to infer that every created soul is immortal and is connected with the universal life-principle of God.

In the higher unfoldment of spiritual law, expression has found a lofty development. One has only to express to himself the desire to be in a certain place, and behold, he is there. He has but to wish to see a particular individual and how he is occupied, and lo! he has brought his friend into his very presence, and the duties with which he is occupied at the time are also shown. Such manifestations can be produced only through intense spirituality and are not to be acquired simply through the desire. The mind of the spirit must be subjected to long and intense thought before the powers mentioned may be attained in any degrees. If it were possible for a person to go into the haunts of nature and remain in one spot for ten or twelve hours, all the while holding in his mind one desire, and not permitting his mind to wander from his subject, he would find himself possessed of a power he never dreamed of before, and the acquirement of one step would prepare him for the next higher one.

Suppose, for instance, he desires the power to leave his body and visit the Spirit World, and then come back and relate what he has seen. He cannot accomplish this by concentrating his mind for a few moments and then have something occur which turns the thought in an entirely different direction.

During the summer months, if one would acquire such powers as have been mentioned, it would be well to seek some quiet woodland spot where one may commune with God and his own soul, as he cannot do amid the hurry and bustle of city life.

Jesus during his earthly career felt often the need of such solace, and when he became weary of the people he would seek some quiet spot, knowing full well that was just what he needed in order to perform his necessary spiritual work. He frequently desired to pray alone and would ask his disciples to leave him, for he was in a state of mind that called for the deep and intense solitude of nature.

The idea seems to be in the minds of people that to be able to leave the physical body is an indication of unbalanced mentality. For this reason many are afraid to subject themselves to any form that will show the higher expression of spiritual law. Because an intelligence possesses the power to lose himself in a physical sense is no indication of insanity, and it is only ignorance that will hold to such an idea. There is a right as well as a wrong idea about these things. The sweet peace and harmony of nature are always conducive to intense spirituality. This is one reason why California furnishes an excellent field for the development of mediumship and its higher laws, because there it seems that one is close to the very soul of nature. There are flowers, birds and soft, balmy air—the soul rejoices and manifests itself as it cannot do in the busy whirl of city life.

In the last few passages written it was shown how one could bring himself into subjection while upon the physical plane, and now to return to the subject of books and writers in the Celestial Sphere.

The writing of T. H. Burgoyne is particularly applicable to those who have passed beyond the primary stages of soul-consciousness and entered into the very soul of things. This is accomplished by different stages of reflection, concentration and spiritual communion with the life-principle which radiates the universe.

The spiritual mind upon the higher plane desires unfoldment, and with desire comes the power. The individual upon the earth plane is not willing to subject himself to those laws by which he may find the power while yet in the physical. *Selfishness is the barrier that holds man back in the physical and prevents him from soaring to the very heights of divine beauty and power.* Even if an individual is of himself unselfish, there are so many selfish vibrations floating about that it is hard for one to keep them off.

The vibrations of the higher world are of a pure, unselfish nature, therefore they cannot strike like keen-pointed arrows into the soul. Only those vibrations which elevate the nature and enable it to grow are received. Therefore there is nothing to hinder spiritual unfoldment in its higher sense.

Prentice Mulford has given a valuable work to the Celestial World. Its title is "The Higher Self in a State of Unfoldment." The author of this work, while in the physical, subjected himself to the dictates of higher law. He could vacate his body and return and also remember what he had seen. When the time came for him to leave the physical, by his wonderful power of mind he simply separated himself from his body while upon one of his long trips. Finding his lifeless body in the boat, the conclusion was that he had passed away from heart failure. It was only that he understood the higher law—that was all.

His passage from the body was a repetition of an act he had often performed, and was as painless as that of a babe lying down to sleep.

Nathaniel Hawthorne has given to the Celestial World a work more weird and fascinating than anything he ever wrote while in the physical. Its title is "Hilda, a Romance of The Celestial Star." It is the tale of a soul born under most peculiar circumstances and of the growth and unfoldment of the spiritual nature of Hilda, how she was betrothed[1] spiritually, while yet unborn, to a twin soul, and how as she grows and develops in the physical world, her spiritual vision remains open and daily she sees and talks with her spiritual affinity, who is an inhabitant of the Celestial World. She does not reveal the peculiar romance of her life to the physical friends, who find in her a character strangely fascinating but not understood.

---

[1] I want to explain to you that there is no marrying nor giving of marriage in Heaven, but all people have a soulmate and the love that exists between these two is purely spiritual. There is no physical law in it. Few people find their soulmates on earth. Some do, and where they do there is only the most perfect harmony existing between the two.

I cannot explain further this intensely interesting book. One who reads it, however, will find nothing but an expression of higher spiritual law.

Thirteen

Music

Music is one of the grandest faculties of the immortal soul. We may say that music is God's voice materialized and made clear to the physical senses. Grand music will lift one to the loftiest heights. The Grand Masters of Music understood well how to touch the divine keys of their soul and thereby produce the exquisite harmonies that will live throughout all time.

All music should possess soul quality, that is, it should not only cause the listener to think of its exquisite tone-harmony, but it should touch the deeper chords of the soul and make him feel the divine touch within that is deeper than all speech, all thought and all expression.

All masters of music must retire as it were to the very sanctuary of the soul and produce the inner harmonies to themselves before they can produce them upon material instruments to delight and inspire the people. Music which is produced from the very depths of the soul will have the effect of bringing the listener close to the divine force within him, and for the time being cause him to forget that there are clouds and trials to be endured.

To produce an immortal symphony, one whose expression will touch the very chords of the soul and cause them to vibrate, one must retire from the things of the world and, for the time being, dwell within the subliminal consciousness which is the mind of the soul. The melodies produced will vibrate upon the finer ear of the spirit and find expression through the physical body in the most inspiring symphonies. In what a rapt state of being must have been Mozart, Beethoven, Wagner, Lizst, Bach, Mendelssohn and other master-composers when they were creating the masterpieces of their souls.

Beautiful music will awaken until they spring into life faculties that have been apparently dormant in the minds of those who have become hardened in the sins of the world. Many a hardened criminal has wept bitter tears upon hearing some simple melody that brought back memories of a time when he was pure and unsullied from contact with the world. It is a fact that if you can reach the soul of an individual through his dense material covering, you can surely influence him for good, and beautiful music is a most potent force in this direction.

It is well for the development of the soul to draw close to nature and attune the ear to her exquisite melodies. The song of the brook, as it dances and plays over the rock, is a most exquisite melody. There is perfect harmony, there is no discord to jar upon the fine, well-trained ear of feeling. The voice of the wind as it sings softly through the trees is a divine symphony from God, and the master soul who can reproduce it upon the keys of an instrument has earned the right to be called "Master of the Keys." As a great writer has said, *"If any man is in doubt as to his identity let him go into the woods and study nature; she will prove to him whether he is a child of God or not."*

To the ear of harmony there is a charm to be found in music that is quite unlike that derived from any of the higher arts, and the man who has music in his soul is capable of being molded in a high degree to that which is in every way desirable. If music was a part of the daily regulations of reformatories, homes for inebriates and insane asylums, it would do a great deal toward subduing the inmates and cause them to become more tractable and easier to manage. It should be the duty of every individual to avail himself of every opportunity within his reach to listen to beautiful grand and soul-inspiring music. It is an educator, not alone of the mental faculties but it furnishes food also for the spiritual in man's nature and causes him to see new beauties in objects hitherto passed by unnoticed.

We may say that the music of the different composers touches different chords in the soul. The music of Wagner touches the chord of fancy and causes the hearer to drift away upon the wings of occasion as light and free as a bird or some merry elf who is simply happy. The music of Beethoven strikes a deeper chord and brings a feeling of grandeur that is quite unlike that produced by any other composer. The music of the different composers touches the chords of sympathy, joy, fancy, grandeur, glory, sadness and love, and the soul that would develop its inner faculties must try to understand the effect of different styles of music upon his nature. If he is by nature light-hearted and fanciful, he must develop the other faculties of his nature and he should therefore cultivate a taste for deep and soulful melodies, that will show him that his soul has mighty depths as well as lofty heights.

The music of the heavenly spheres is upon a much grander and more beautiful scale than that afforded the soul in its material environment. It is music for the unfolded soul. Beethoven's divine symphony, Handel's "Eternal Rhapsodic" and Wagner's "Music of the Spheres and Plan of Creation," and Handel's "Celestial Chorus," are all compositions of a very high order and may well be classified as masterpieces of divine melody, and the souls of those privileged to participate in such grand performances as those which take place in the heavenly spheres are indeed in tune with the infinite of life in the divine.

Fourteen

Inspiration

There are times when the souls of philosophers and deep thinkers are attuned to the vibrations of inspiring angels who surround them, and at such times the eloquence is soulful and creates an impression upon the hearers as nothing else can. The soul is like a sweet-toned harp that vibrates beneath the touch of a master's hand, but mute and expressionless under an unfavorable influence.

The power to be inspired is a gift from God Himself—it is divine. Therefore, the soul should endeavor to place itself in an attitude that will invite inspiration. The gifted artist as he stands before his canvas is conscious of a lofty, uplifted feeling, and lo, his hand is guided to portray a masterly conception that angelic friends have impressed upon his soul. He paints with a skill and cunning he never was conscious of before. While angelic minds have produced the impression upon his soul, angel-hands have sent out electric vibrations that have guided his hands to produce those wonderful tints and shadings of color, so remarkable to the eye of the beholder.

Many of the old Masters were inspired, and while producing their work have been within the Temple of the Soul. They withdrew from the world, as it were, and communion with the angelic friends who have come to meet them. They have shut out all worldly thoughts and influences, and only the sublime creations and fancies of, another world have found an entrance.

The soul of the inspired man is in tune with the Infinite. As he looks within himself he sees a mighty illumination that lights up the whole interior of his being, and there at the divine center, the seat of the soul, he sees the beautiful thoughts of angelic friends flowing in through the power of vibration—he lets them rest for a moment upon the altar seat and then brings them into his brain, and they come forth through his mouth in grand and sublime conceptions of beauty. If he is a musician they come through his hands. If he is an inspirational speaker, they come through his lips. If a writer, they come directly from his soul to find expression through his fingers.

The soul who desires the gift of inspiration must cultivate his spiritual nature and make himself receptive to the influence of his angelic friends. If he reads the works of gifted authors, he will put himself in a condition receptive to the influence of such intelligences as Henry Ward Beecher, Phillips Brooks, Longfellow, Whittier, Tennyson, Holmes, Emerson, as well as many others too numerous to mention. Of course he may make himself receptive to a particular style by making a life study of one particular master of thought. The thoughts that come through his soul will be clothed in his own original language, but will have the style and peculiarity of his favorite writer.

Myron W. Reed was a great admirer of Ralph Waldo Emerson, and Emerson was like a teacher to him. At the same time, while his thoughts were his own, yet they were expressed in the style of Emerson and he was called the Emerson of the West.

Grand and beautiful, masterly in conception are the thoughts of angelic visitants from the celestial world.

Many times when attempting to inspire a gifted mind they find that their ideas are so far in advance of the people to whom they would speak that the real beauty and majesty of the thought falls upon soil not yet ready for the mighty revelation of a higher and better world.

Inspiration is carried on in different ways. The great inventor, Edison, is met by gifted scientists from the higher world immediately after vacating his body during the period of sleep. They repair to some chosen place, either to his laboratory or to the scientific halls of the Spirit World. He is then shown just how to work out some particular line or point of an invention he is working upon in the physical. The law of suggestion is applied to him, and Professor Faraday asks him to go into deep silence within his laboratory upon the following day at a given hour. After he is shown some intricate part, he leaves them, returns to his body and wakes up. Sometimes the complete plan of the work and all that has passed during the night will be remembered—then again he will not remember, but exactly at 5:30 or 6 o'clock, the hour that was suggested to him, he retires into his laboratory and gives himself up to deeper thought, and he plans out what he should do to complete some new arrangement in his invention. He suddenly sees just what he should do and he goes to work upon it and it goes forth into the world a work that causes people to marvel and say what a wonderful man is Edison.

The scientific men from the higher world are at work continually upon some invention that is going to make the material world better and upon a more improved plan. Edward Bellamy, who wrote "Looking Backward," begins to see the realization of certain improvements mentioned in his book. He is happy because of this. It would interest the people of earth could they visit some of the extensive laboratories in the higher world and the great work of invention going on. The world should rejoice that it has the God-given power of inspiration, for it is the work of inspiration, brought down from Heaven by the angels of God, that will cause the material plane to send forth fruit and blossom like the rose.

All things work together for good to them that love God.

ST. PAUL.

Thou shalt love thy neighbor as thyself.

JESUS.

Ye shall know the truth, and the truth shall make you free.

JESUS.

Fifteen

New Thought Movement

The mind of man is continually soaring upward to the most sublime heights of glory. Through the power of the new thought, the very gates of Heaven swing open to receive him. The book of immortality is opened before him, and upon its inspired pages he may find the keynote to the most forceful and intricate of life's problems. Like the bright winged butterfly emerging from its ugly chrysalis does the new thought, sparkling with a thousand iridescent dyes, emerge from the somber garments of the old thought. From east to west, from north to south, from empire to empire, it shall wing its way into the palaces of the rich and favored of humanity and into the hovels of the poor. The mighty power of thought shall prove the conquest of many things. You cannot prune the wings of thought during these enlightened days, for through its mighty powers shall the world be made to blossom like the rose and flourish like the bay tree.

In those realms of light beyond the earth, the power of thought is developed and unfolded to that extent that it has only to desire the creation or completion of a work, and behold, it appears clothed in the glory and strength of mighty power. The mind of man is gradually working toward this end upon the material plane, and when that mind learns to cast off its shackles of selfishness, the world and all of its powers may be his. Universal brotherhood shall prove the conquest of poverty. More love and charity shall be the solution to crime and its conqueror. Education and the understanding of hereditary and parental law shall overcome the curse of ignorance.

The new thought movement shall teach men the shame of ignorance; for ignorance and poverty are the parents of crime, and must be banished as things of the past, for which the new [20th] century will have no use. Oh, my friends, look into your souls; bring forth the jewel of thought. Does its luster appear to be dim? Then polish it up and make it beautiful, for it is the philosopher's stone of the new century. You do not dream of its powers nor of what you may accomplish through its development.

The spiritual mind in a developed state can by the power of thought draw together the elements and particles to produce a beautiful picture; by the exercise of thought it can produce writing in the atmosphere, or upon substances without the exercise of the arm or hand. The spiritual mind can send out a vibratory thought and produce raps without the contact of the person with any visible substance.

It is well for one to understand that by his own mind he may project visible writing into the atmosphere. The strength that grows from this will help him to produce something stronger and more beautiful. There are creations in the spiritual world that have been produced by spiritual beings solely through the powers of thought. Those who believe that thought is limited in its power of expression are laboring under a mistaken idea. The more thought is developed the stronger it may become. A mighty development of thought power will enable one to project his spiritual being to the higher world and return again to his physical body. This power, of course, is one of the higher stages and will come after growth.

The spiritual being in a highly developed stage of thought can send its particles out into the atmosphere all but the ego, or divine center, which emanates from God, and can by another exercise bring together those particles until they form the same appearance as before.

One who would perform miraculous powers of thought should study well the laws of chemistry and perform experiments with different chemicals.

The beautiful elements of thought are situated in the front part and on the center of head. He who desires a development of beautiful thought must center his mind upon those points just over his eyes and across the top of the head. Constant attention to this point will cause them to expand and develop.

Force is located just above the ears on each side of the head. One in developing this must be careful not to exercise that part too much, for by so doing he may go beyond that which is merely forceful and develop combativeness, or brute strength.

The development of physical strength is located in the back part of the head, and here one must be also careful, or he will go beyond that which is necessary to round out the beautiful character of man. One cannot center his thought power upon those parts situated in the top and center of the head; for there is spirituality centered, and the divine center of life, into which flows the spiritual vibrations from the creator of life.

When one gives himself up to thought he should understand how to center himself in order to produce the most effectual results. Wandering around from one point to another in the brain, or in the soul, is not good unless one has first devoted a certain number of minutes to the different points that he would develop. He must not forget while in his physical body that if he develops so many new degrees of spirituality he must at the same time develop at least one degree of physical strength, or he will find his spiritual nature growing so rapidly that he will have difficulty to hold it down to the earth. In other words, he will become so spiritual that the thread of life which holds the soul in the physical can be very easily snapped, and he may go out to the other world as easily as lying down to sleep. There are some who really desire this intense spirituality of nature, and if they cultivate it they can of course acquire it.

The mental attributes in the center and front part of the head lie not far from the surface of the brain. The spiritual mental attributes are deeper in to the center, and one must learn to penetrate the gray matter into the deeper center if he would come in touch with the higher within him. The individual would be surprised at the great depth within, for the outer envelopes seem to expand as one penetrates within. Man can make it seem as though he himself was walking about at full height in the chambers of his own brain or soul. This understanding comes only through practice and by persistent effort, and no man need attempt it until he has accustomed himself to the primary stages of retrospection and reflection. Each step must be well learned in the solution of the great problem of thought.

The works of today that are accomplished through the power of thought will be looked upon as mere pygmies in the centuries to come in comparison to what will be accomplished. In the years to come no telegraph or telephone will be needed, nor will people be obliged to send letters through the mail. Thought will accomplish this in a much more effectual manner, for the transmitter who desires to send word to his friend thousands of miles away will only need to send out a vibration to that friend, and he will immediately put himself in the position as receiver and will receive the messages in a more satisfactory manner than he can now do through the telephone or by letter.

Better it would be for man to expend his force upon the wonderful yet undeveloped power within him than upon the wireless telegraph or other like achievements. The time is not far distant when man will learn to center instead of scattering his force. He has the power within him, and if he only knew it he would not be obliged to go out of himself to find power to work out his plans. The force is lying dormant but ready at the touch of a quickening hand to spring forth into mighty life, to overcome all obstacles and soar upward into the very heights of sublime conception.

A man or woman developed in the mighty power of thought is a conqueror, and to them the unseen world shall sing "Ride on, Ride on to Glory." With unfurled banners floating, proudly on the wind, ye have the solution to life's problems and are conquerors in your own right.

Sixteen

Trinity

The Fatherhood of God, the Brotherhood of Man, and the Fellowship of the Holy Ghost—these constitute the Trinity, Three in One and One in Three. The Universal Power which extends throughout all Nature, Spiritual and Material, constitutes the Fatherhood of God. Every man is a part of the Father. Every plant that grows and every animate and inanimate thing which is, is an expression of the Most High, and is a spark from the Divine; and the Great Father of Nature has set his seal upon them all, and they breathe of his wisdom and mighty power.

In the Fatherhood of God we find eternal and immortal power, a center of supply that flows out to man and to the expressions of all nature. Life is a force which may not be destroyed in the change called death. There is only a separation of the life-cells, and that which seems dead to material eyes will soon begin to take up its work in nature.

The air is filled with particles that only a short time ago were parts of an apparently inanimate object. The Universal

Life Principle is the force which emanates from the center of all life in God's Kingdom in the world above. This force radiating through all forms of life constitutes the Fatherhood of God.

"Worship My Son and ye worship Me, for He is the light which emanates from Me." This refers to Jesus, the most spiritual type of man and the nearest to the Father. Men should look upon him as God's highest expression and as an example of how one should live in order to gain the highest, the purest and best in life.

The Soul of Man constitutes the third part of the Trinity. For in a highly developed state of spirituality a man may realize his connection with the Most High by a state of exalted feeling, which helps to illuminate his Spiritual Temple, and causes him to experience that peace which passeth understanding, and brings him in tune with the Infinite. The world is gradually drawing nearer to a more comprehensive understanding of the Trinity, God the Father, Jesus the Son, and the connecting vibrations, which unite with the Soul of Man, bring the Three into One, and thus constitute the Trinity, Three in One and One in Three, Father, Son and Holy Ghost, or Spirit of God making itself manifest in Man's Spiritual Temple, when he is in tune with the higher understanding.

Seventeen

The Holy Ghost

The time has come when the masses should understand the vital questions, the solution of which means so much in the progress and development of the soul. The Holy Ghost and the sin against it is a subject not properly understood, and spiritual teachers from the higher realms of life propose to make this subject clear in the minds of men. What is the Holy Ghost? The solution must come first before the crime against it may be understood. The Holy Ghost is the Spirit of God made manifest in the human soul. It is not God afar off, it is God in the soul. The presence of the Holy Ghost within the soul fills the whole being with a strange and wonderful peace. It is that peace which passeth understanding and lifts the soul up until it is in touch with the divine center of all life forces.

The Holy Spirit of God is of that strange and mighty power that it may, through desire, at once find an abiding place within. Its presence is made known by divine vibrations that connect with the God principle that dwells within the soul. Therefore, the Holy Ghost is the spirit of God made manifest at that point known as the God principle, in *the soul*, the inheritance of the Father to the children of His love and care.

The sin against the Holy Ghost is the denial of the soul by the physical nature. That force which rejects the higher attributes and refuses to develop them is a crime, it is a sin against God, for those higher forces are of God and should be strengthened, unfolded and made to grow. Instead of doing this, the physical uses the force to develop its faculties, while the God principle is ignored in every way except that demand that gives life to the body. The physical becomes the matter instead of the spiritual, and finally the physical nature becomes so callous to the promptings of the soul that it never thinks of such a possession as a higher nature. When this occurs, the Holy Ghost may enter the soul, but the door between the physical and spiritual is so tightly locked and barred that the individual never realizes that he has had a visit from a *divine guest*. Those higher occurrences are as foreign to him as though they had never occurred. Such an individual never begins to work out his salvation until he has laid aside his physical body. He moves along through life unconscious of the fact that he daily commits a sin against God, the Creator and giver of all life.

All through man's life two principles work for good or for evil—the human and the divine. Instead of developing harmoniously together the human and the spiritual, they are separated, as it were, in their likes and dislikes. The spiritual vibrations which emanate from the God of light and love to a receptive soul fill the whole being with an indescribable sensation. It is the very acme of intense divine feeling, and is quite unlike any physical sensation that can be experienced. All men should love to cultivate the divine principle within the human soul, and in that way make it receptive to the influence of the

Holy Ghost, and an understanding of this fact will make the efforts to gain success comparatively easy, and conquest after conquest will be gained with but very little exertion. Some people will call this conquest luck, when it is the unseen force from within vibrating upon the minds of those with whom the person comes in context. This silent force will cause those who come near the individual to suddenly feel an indefinable something that is of the nature of peace or extreme delight. It will cause a horse to turn his head as the person passes him. The more this force is cultivated the stronger and more potent does it become. Jesus had this force, and the God principle manifesting itself through him drew men to him, while others whose natures were very dense could see nothing desirable in him or in his power. They were the individuals who had developed the physical nature and let the God principle remain dormant. The wonders that may be brought about through the development of this force that exists in the very depths of nature are not known, much less understood by the individual of today. If they only were the world would be a more harmonious place to live in, and a great deal that is falsely interpreted by Bible teachings might be made clear. The unpleasant things of life would be no longer attributed to God, and their source could be traced back to a purely physical cause. We say that the sin against the Holy Ghost is the greatest evil, for from it arise the sin, crime, poverty, selfishness and pain of the world. *If man would learn to commune with the higher source of life all of these evils would be done away with.*

I have heard church people say, "We know it is a crime to sin against the Holy Ghost, but we don't understand what the sin is." How necessary that spiritual teachers should possess the knowledge of a truth before they attempt to impart it to others, and yet there are few ministers who understand the

Trinity, the Plan of Salvation, the Holy Ghost, or the Peace that passeth understanding. They can tell you what they think it is, but as for the absolute knowledge, they do not possess it. They have been taught to believe that it is wrong to reason out such things. If reason were contrary to the mind of the Creator, why did he give to man the faculty which seeks to reason out things? Where would the world be today in knowledge and achievement if the great force of reason had not been put to an active use? When men cease to reason for themselves there will be no growth. Man will stop right where he is, content to believe that everything that exists or is made is perfect of itself and requires no change. Let us rejoice to know that reason has come to stay, and the theory that has not reason for its foundation will not exist for long, for the people of today demand a reasonable age. Those truths of the Bible which have reason for their foundation have come to stay, while those that will not bear analysis will be rejected as mere figures of speech, with no divine principle within them. A new Bible of reason shall be written, and in it shall be explained in a clearer light those things which the average mind has so far been unable to assimilate. The idea that a sacrifice of blood and torture would be pleasing to a God who is supposed to possess attributes above the mind of man will be another unreasonable idea that will be done away with, since every man must work out his own salvation, and not by the blood of Christ shall ye be saved.

How much more beautiful to think that the gentle Jesus came to show men an example of a purely spiritual being with the better forces of the spiritual nature developed than to think that His death was ordained by a loving father—a death that a human parent could not endure to see the child of his life suffer.

Let every man reason for himself. Let him learn that he may become the abiding place of God if he will; that he may be lifted up until the higher laws may be made manifest unto him, and the golden gates of Heaven may swing wide open to receive him at such times when he desires to center his force upon those higher truths which well understood may bring Heaven down to earth to the music of the Divine Symphony.

Eighteen

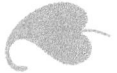

A Treatise on Molecules

All forms of created life are evolved from a molecule. A molecule need not necessarily be an inert particle of matter, since in order for it to grow and move it must possess force, and force is life. A molecule in its primary sense must consist in the union of the two forces, positive and negative, and from this union will growth result, whether it be in the vegetable, mineral, animal or human. In every living molecule is a tiny spark of electrical force. This united with the magnetic force of nature causes growth and evolution.

A molecule of the human system is threefold in its nature. It consists of matter which is magnetic; spirit, which is electrical; and mind, which is the force of attraction between matter and spirit and which holds them together. When a molecule is thrown off from the physical system, it loses the individuality of the human and through the law of chemical nature is transformed into some other expression of nature.

A molecule, however infinitesimal to the ordinary vision, may be described as a circle within a circle with a tiny spark of evolving force within its center. This spark of evolving force is positive in its nature, and it draws unto itself those elements which are necessary for its sustenance and growth.

The study of molecules should show the human being why he should keep his organism in a healthful condition, and instead of throwing off molecules of disease he should give out only that which is true, healthful and good. The atmosphere is impregnated at all times with molecules which differ in their constituent elements, but which, nevertheless, are the result of the union of the two forces, positive and negative. It is quite essential that the human individual comprehend the molecular law. In the creation of life in the human, the minute individual is a molecule, and within that molecule are folded away not alone his individual parts in a very minute sense, but infinitesimal parts of future generations. According to this law, the human molecule is of far greater importance than it is given by the average individual.

Microbes are molecules of disease. They have not the spiritual center of the molecules spoken of elsewhere.

The human system is daily throwing off particles which are replaced by new ones. These new ones may be healthy or diseased. It all depends upon the care that the individual exercises in relation to his own organism. If his system is diseased he attracts diseased molecules, and thereby increases the inharmony in his system, and vice versa.

A human molecule consists of three parts, while that of a vegetable or mineral only two. They also vary in their constituent elements. It has been said that matter of itself does not possess life, yet plants and minerals which are nature's matter grow, and growth is the expression of life. In the condition called death the molecules which constituted the physical and mental system became separated as it were, since the mighty law of attraction which held them together has been evolved into a higher expression of godly love.

We may say that a molecule is the effect of a cause. The cause was the union of the two forces, positive and negative, from which has been evolved the human physical, the magnetic mental and the electrical spiritual. This evolution from cause to effect constitutes the grandest and highest expression of the creator.

Upon analysis of the creative molecule within the individual we may discover the tiniest forms of inherited tendency both of good and evil, that have existed in some ancestor of this individual perhaps two generations back. How essential, then, that the law of inheritance should be understood. In the creative molecule of an individual of today may be the seed of disease or evil that will be discovered perhaps three hundred years from this date. This explains the passage in the Bible: "The sins of the father shall descend into the children of the third and fourth generation." Few have thought to trace a hereditary disease or a grievous tendency to commit wrong down to a tiny molecule, that in appearance is an inert particle of matter; but the people of today sow the tiny seed or molecule of good within their own physical system, the seed which holds within itself a still smaller seed and within this smaller seed one still more infinitesimal, and there at the very root will be discovered the tiny germ which is the beginning of another life which will be in existence many years from this present date November 26, 1902.

We have good reason to believe that an invention will yet be given to the world whose magnifying powers will enable the human eye to discover in the interior functions of the male and female element the life-germs or molecules of future generations, folded closely within many circles of matter or positive and negative force.

Nineteen

A Christmas Sermon to Humanity

At Christmastime it is well for all people to give some time to reflection, to turn back the pages of life's book just one year, and to read that which has been inscribed upon the pages.

In that way one may be able to determine the progress he has made during the year. It will also give him time to think of the new, clean book he is to be given upon the first day of the year, and of how he is going to write upon its pages. Bear in mind that life is a book and a page is turned at the close of every day.

On Christmas day let the holiday spirit reign. Think of those less fortunate than yourself and send them helpful thoughts and vibrations if you can send them nothing more. Utter the thought to yourself: I will do what I can. A kindly thought or a cup of cold water given in love is pleasing to the angels of heaven who can see all that goes on in the material world. Upon Christmas wish much good for humanity. Pray that man may understand that he is a free agent. And since he himself is the creator of sin, disease and inharmony, also poverty, he may by his own creative power create their opposite—good, love, prosperity and universal brotherhood.

Pray that he may understand that selfishness and ignorance are the parents of crime, and whosoever fosters them works against the higher law of universal good.

Upon Christmas day enter into the sanctuary of your souls, and commune with the God within you. It is easy enough to determine after doing this whether you are doing a good or a poor work in the way you are serving humanity.

Frame these words in your mind and hang them in the art gallery of your soul: Peace on the earth, good will to men. If you will do this you will feel better satisfied with yourself at the close of the day.

Since Christmas is the saddest and the happiest day of all the year, try to find some compensation for the sad memories that will come up in spite of yourself. If a dear one who was with you a year ago has passed beyond the Valley of the Shadow, think of him as having found a fairer and brighter home in the beautiful beyond. Think of him as being with you, occupying the chair which has seemed to you in your ignorance to be so vacant; think that all is well with him, he has only passed to a higher school of understanding and it is only because you are not sufficiently advanced in spiritual understanding to be able to understand the wisdom and mighty power of the most high who ordereth all things well.

Let your Christmas day be one step in advance upon the pathway of light that leads to immortal life. Ask that God give you light and spiritual illumination until the mighty *principles* which govern spiritual law be clearly manifest unto you; that you may say no longer "I believe," but rather, "I know. I have the knowledge; it hath been revealed unto me that the soul of man continues after the change called death. That it continues to grow and unfold its beautiful powers throughout all eternity, and that it continues to hold its individuality throughout all time. That the soul of man is progressive, that it was not created to go back into any lower form, but to climb upward and onward, and to unfold in the beautiful sunlight of God's smile."

Such thoughts as these are helpful upon Christmas day and at all times for their creation will help to strengthen the spiritual.

Think of the gentle teacher the anniversary of whose birth is celebrated upon this day. He understood the higher law and was able to demonstrate it from this fact alone, and not on account of any miraculous birth, but because he was at all times spiritually-minded and much given to inward thought and reflection. Through his spirituality he developed certain senses that are dormant in the average individual, consequently man is unable to perform certain works that the gentle teacher of Nazareth gave unto the world.

It is well for any individual of ordinary comprehension to try and understand the full and complete meaning of the higher thought, remembering that it is the assimilating of such thoughts that will furnish food for his soul nature.

The individual should be in tune with himself. Upon Christmas day he should listen to the divine symphony of his own soul that is being rendered within his own spiritual Temple.

A Merry Christmas.

December 25, 1902.

www.ingramcontent.com/pod-product-compliance
Lightning Source LLC
Chambersburg PA
CBHW022115040426
42450CB00006B/716